9-16

World Economics Association
Book Series
Volume 5

Green Capitalism
The God that Failed

D1572672

DISCARD

Titles produced by the World Economics Association & College Publications

Volume 1
The Economics Curriculum: Towards a Radical reformulation
Maria Alejandra Maki and Jack Reardon, eds.

Volume 2
Finance as Warfare
Michael Hudson

Volume 3
Developing an economics for the post-crisis world
Steve Keen

Volume 4
On the use and misuse of theories and models in mainstream economics
Lars Pålsson Syll

Volume 5
Green Capitalism. The God that Failed
Richard Smith

The **World Economics Association (WEA)** was launched on May 16, 2011. Already over 13,000 economists and related scholars have joined. This phenomenal success has come about because the WEA fills a huge gap in the international community of economists – the absence of a professional organization which is truly international and pluralist.

The World Economics Association seeks to increase the relevance, breadth and depth of economic thought. Its key qualities are worldwide membership and governance, and inclusiveness with respect to: (a) the variety of theoretical perspectives; (b) the range of human activities and issues which fall within the broad domain of economics; and (c) the study of the world's diverse economies.

The Association's activities centre on the development, promotion and diffusion of economic research and knowledge and on illuminating their social character.

The WEA publishes 20+ books a year, three open-access journals (*Economic Thought*, *World Economic Review* and *Real-World Economics Review*), a bi-monthly newsletter, blogs, holds global online conferences, runs a textbook commentaries project and an eBook library.

www.worldeconomicassociation.org

Green Capitalism
The God that Failed

Richard Smith

© Richard Smith, WEA and College Publications 2016.

All rights reserved.

ISBN 978-1-84890-205-3 print
ISBN 978-1-911156-22-2 eBook-PDF

Published by College Publications on behalf of the World Economics Association

http://www.worldeconomicsassociation.org
http://www.collegepublications.co.uk

Cover photograph. CG Imaging by John Blackford / Photography by Cameron Davidson

Printed by Lightning Source, Milton Keynes, UK

For Nancy and Alexandra
and the better world we dream of

Contents

Introduction

This book is a collection of five essays that deal with the prime threat to human life on Earth: the tendency of global capitalist economic development to develop us to death, to drive us off the cliff to ecological collapse. It begins with a review of the origins of this economic dynamic in the transition to capitalism in England and Europe and with an analysis of the ecological implications of capitalist economics as revealed in the work of its founding theorist – Adam Smith. I argue that, once installed, the requirements of reproduction under capitalism – the pressure of competition, the imperative need to innovate and develop the forces of production to beat the competition, the need to constantly grow production and expand the market and so on, induced an expansive logic that has driven economic development and overdevelopment, down to the present day.

In successive essays I explicate and criticize the two leading mainstream approaches to dealing with the ecological consequences of this over-developmental dynamic – *décroisance* or "degrowth", and "green capitalism". I show that the theorists and proponents of no-growth or de-growth – like Herman Daly or Tim Jackson – are correct in arguing that infinite economic growth is not possible on a finite planet, but that they're wrong to imagine that capitalism can be refashioned as a kind of "steady state" economy, let alone actually "degrow" without precipitating economic collapse. There are further problems with this model, which I also investigate. I show that the theorists and proponents of "green capitalism" such as Paul Hawkin, Lester Brown and Frances Cairncross are wrong to think that tech miracles, "dematerialization", new efficiencies, recycling and the like, will permit us to grow the global economy – more or less forever – without consuming and polluting ourselves to death. I show that while we're all better off with organic groceries, energy-efficient light bulbs and so on, such developments do not fundamentally reverse the eco-suicidal tendencies of capitalist development, because in any capitalist economy the environment has to be subordinated to maximizing growth and sales, or companies can't survive in the marketplace. Yet infinite growth, even green growth, is impossible on a finite planet.

Green capitalism: the god that failed

In the final essays I argue that since capitalism can only drive us to ecological collapse, we have no choice but to try to cashier this system and replace it with an entirely different economy and mode of life based on: minimizing not maximizing resource consumption; public ownership of most, though not necessarily all, of the economy; large-scale economic planning and international coordination; and a global "contraction and convergence" between the North and the South around a lower but hopefully satisfactory level of material consumption for all the world's peoples. Whether we can pull off such a transition is another question. We may very well fail to overthrow capitalism and replace it with a viable alternative. That may be our fate. But around the world, in thousands of locations, people are organizing and fighting against corporate power, against land grabs, against extreme extraction, against the incessant commodification of our lives. Here and there, as in Greece and China, ruling classes are on the defensive. All these fights have a common demand: bottom-up democracy, popular power. In this lies our best hope. This little book is intended as more ammunition for that fight.

A note on the texts

Three of the five essays in this book were published previously as articles in *Real-World Economics Review* since 2010. Essay 1 is based on my article "The eco-suicidal economics of Adam Smith" which appeared in *Capitalism Nature Socialism* 18:2 (2007). Essay 4 was first published in *truthout.org* on November 12, 2014.

About the author

Richard Smith has worked as a sailboat rigger, trans-Africa adventure travel leader, carpenter / builder and briefly as a lecturer in history. He wrote his UCLA History Ph.D. thesis on the contradictions of market reform in China's transition to capitalism (1989). He held postdoctoral appointments at the East-West Center in Honolulu and at Rutgers University New Brunswick and has published articles on the Chinese revolution, China's road to capitalism, and capitalist development and China's environment for *Against the Current, New Left Review,* the *Ecologist,* and *Monthly Review* and other journals. He has published articles on capitalism and the global ecological crisis in the *Journal of Ecological Economics, Capitalism Nature Socialism, Real-World Economics Review, Truthout.org, Adbusters,* and other media. He is presently completing a book on China's ecological apocalypse (Verso 2017).

Introduction

Acknowledgements

First of all, I want to thank Robert Brenner my thesis supervisor and friend who taught me Marxist theory and history. I want to thank my wife Nancy Holmstrom for her untiring encouragement, perceptive advice, and patience. And here I especially want to thank Edward Fullbrook who has enthusiastically supported my work from the first paper I submitted in April 2010 and who conceived this book.

Green capitalism: the god that failed

ESSAY 1 (2007)

How did the common good become a bad idea? The eco-suicidal economics of Adam Smith

In the midst of the record-breaking heat wave of summer 2003, George Monbiot, the renowned columnist for the London *Guardian,* penned a short but eloquent essay entitled "Sleepwalking to Extinction". Monbiot wrote that:

> "We live in a dream world. With a small, rational part of our brain, we recognise that our existence is... destroying the conditions for human life on earth. Were we governed by reason, we would be on the barricades today, dragging the drivers of Range Rovers and Nissan Patrols out of their seats, occupying and shutting down the coal-burning power stations, bursting in upon the Blairs' retreat from reality in Barbados and demanding a reversal of economic life as dramatic as the one we bore when we went to war with Hitler" (*Guardian*, August 12, 2003).

But despite the frightening trends, despite ever more desperate pleas from the world's scientists, the world's corporate and political leadership shows no sign of abandoning denial and adopting "reason", no sign of scrapping business-as-usual to mobilize against catastrophe. The ritual has now become depressingly familiar and predictable: after each new "shocking" report on melting icecaps, the slowing Gulf Stream current, eco-devastation in Africa or China, and so on, "concerned" politicians call for "immediate action" and "drastic steps" – then do nothing at all of substance.

Since the first conference in Rio in 1992, every December UN Climate Convention negotiations summit talks begin with urgent pleas from devastated communities from poorer countries and expert scientists, then collapse in rancor and disarray over the failure of nations to accept binding limits on greenhouse gas emissions. At every turn, the priority of growth and profits overrides every ringing fire alarm, and society carries on in its "sleepwalk to extinction". In the 2006 rehearsal of this charade, the UN Nairobi summit collapsed into nothingness with no firm targets adopted, nothing concrete agreed and every issue of any seriousness postponed yet again. Kofi Annan decried the assembled ministers as "frighteningly timid", "lacking in leadership", displaying "a failure of political will". One Greenpeace observer remarked that "the glaciers in Greenland are moving faster than the negotiators".[1] The November Nairobi Climate Convention talks came just after Britain's treasury secretary and former World Bank Chief Economist Sir Nicholas Stern sounded the alarm with his blistering six-hundred-page report laying down a challenge to Britain and the United States, as well as developing nations like China and India, that the planet faces imminent catastrophe unless urgent measures are taken to reduce greenhouse emissions immediately. Stern's warning went beyond restating an apocalyptic vision of hundreds of millions fleeing flooding and drought, and struck at the heart of the corporate resistance to environmental measures by demonstrating that the cost of inaction could be the permanent loss of perhaps 20 percent of global output while the cost of preventive action right then could have been, on his accounting, as little as 1 to 2 percent of GNP. This should have knocked the last leg out from under the "environment versus economy" argument by demonstrating the huge *economic* cost that inaction will impose, even on the industrialized economies. Reiterating the conclusions of the UN IPCC scientists, Stern warned that just to stabilize CO_2 and other greenhouse gases in the atmosphere at between 450 and 500 parts per million (the last time the planet experienced CO_2 levels as high as 500ppm was twenty to forty million years ago and sea levels were 100 meters higher than today), we will have to cut global emissions by 25 percent and cut wealthy-country emissions by 60 percent by the year 2050. Presenting the findings in London, the then Prime Minister, Tony Blair, said the consequences of inaction were "literally disastrous" and warned that: "This disaster is not set to happen in some science fiction future many years ahead in our lifetime. We can't wait the five years it took to negotiate Kyoto – we simply don't have the time. Without radical measures to reduce carbon dioxide emissions in the next 10 to 15 years, there is compelling evidence to suggest that we might lose the chance to control temperature rises."[2] The Stern report came just as the International Energy Agency announced that China, which was commissioning a new coal-fired power

[1] Xan Rice, "Little Progress at Climate Summit," *Guardian*, November 18, 2006; Jeffrey Gettleman, "Annan Faults 'Frightening Lack of Leadership' for Global Warming," *New York Times*, November 16, 2006; Andrew C. Revkin, "Talks to Start on Climate amid Split on Warming," *New York Times*, November 5, 2006.
[2] Colin Brown and Rupert Cornwall, "The Day That Changed the Climate," *Independent*, October 31, 2006; Larry Elliott and Patrick Wintour, "Stern Review Prompts Britain to Seek Global Climate Deal," *Guardian Weekly*, November 3–9, 2006.

How did the common good become a bad idea?

plant every five days, surpassed the United States in 2009 as the world's biggest emitter of carbon dioxide. Largely because of China's growth, the Global Carbon Project reported in the November 13, 2006 issue of *Nature* that:

> "Global carbon emissions are now growing by 3.2% a year... That's four times higher than the average annual growth of 0.8% from 1990–1999... We are not on any of the stabilization paths."

Professor Bill McGuire, director of the Benfield Hazard Research Centre in London, said:

> "This is more very bad news. We need a 60 to 70 per cent cut in emissions, but instead, emission levels are spiraling out of control. The sum total of our meager efforts to cut emissions amounts to less than zero."[3]

So then, what sort of "radical measures to reduce carbon dioxide emissions in the next 10 to 15 years" did Blair and Stern propose to stop this onrushing catastrophe? Unsurprisingly, they proposed *no* radical measures, *no* draconian legislation against pollution, not even a call for mandatory limits on emissions – which they specifically rejected as "too inflexible". Most critically, Stern and Blair failed to confront the implications of inexorable growth. After all their rhetoric about impending catastrophe, the best they could do was call for more "carbon pricing", "more research into new technologies" and "robust international agreements". Blair was immediately chastised by his own party for resisting binding targets.[4] After all, carbon pricing schemes, where they had been tried, notably in the European Union, had already conspicuously failed as economic growth just barreled right through the Kyoto carbon "limits". And what possible technical breakthroughs could cut global CO_2 emissions by 60 to 70 percent the 10- to 15-year timeframe Blair said we had to act when new coal-fired power plants were being built not only in China and India but even the United States?[5] Even as efficiency gains were growing and even as

[3] Quoted in Steve Connor, "Global Growth in Carbon Emissions Is 'Out of Control,' *Independent*, November 12, 2006.
[4] Larry Elliot and Patrick Wintour, "Stern Review Prompts Britain to Seek Global Climate Deal," *Guardian Weekly*, November 3–9, 2006; Nigel Morris, "Blair Faces Revolt over CO_2 Targets," *Independent*, November 13, 2006.
[5] Just one utility in Texas alone planned to build eleven coal-fired plants by 2010. Matthew L. Wald, "Committed to Coal, and in a Hurry, Too," *New York Times*, November 7, 2006.

7

more sophisticated pollution controls were installed on cars and power plants, these gains were regularly outstripped by ever-growing production, with the result that throughout the 2000s, CO_2 emissions were soaring.[6] And CO_2 emissions are only one of the looming ecological catastrophes we face. Around the world, forests are vanishing, clean water is disappearing, coral reefs are dying off, species after species are being driven to extinction, resource after resource is being exhausted – everywhere, the natural world is being relentlessly sacrificed to the god of growth and profits.[7]

Blair's hypocrisy followed a long-established pattern. At every point, he and his ministers sacrificed the environment for growth. In 2005, Blair's chief minister and designated successor Gordon Brown even called for "scrapping" the United Kingdom's Kyoto targets despite Labour's manifesto pledges since 1997 to reach those targets. In May 2006, Blair told a climate conference in New Zealand that "I don't want it on the conscience of me, or my generation, that we were told what this problem was and did nothing about it." He then turned around and refused to back the 58-point program put forward by his own environment secretary Margaret

---

[6] John Vidal, "American Global Warming Gas Emissions Accelerate to a Record High," *Independent*, December 22, 2005. For example, the Matsushta Electric TOP Panasonic Report for Sustainability 2005 notes that "In Japan, fiscal 2005 CO_2 emissions per actual unit of production improved by 16 percent compared to fiscal 1991. Even so, CO_2 emissions in Japan increased by 330,000 tons, to 1.95 million tons, compared to fiscal 1991. This increase is attributable to expanded production volume in the device division, including semiconductors and plasma display panels (PDPs). Demand is exploding for digital home appliances, and the heart of these appliances is PDPs and semiconductors such as system LSIs. The microfabrication process for semiconductor wafers and the manufacture of panels for PDPs require large amounts of energy. Future CO_2 emissions can therefore be expected to increase along with the continuing expansion of these businesses." See http://panasonic.co.jp/eco/en/rpt2005/env02_02.html. A report in the United Kingdom suggested that "The domestic boom in flatscreen TVs" could pump as much as 700,000 tons of extra carbon into the atmosphere each year, hampering Britain's attempt to cut emissions. Ben Russell, "Flat Screen Televisions 'Will Add to Global Warming,'" *Independent*, November 1, 2006.
[7] E.g. Ian Sample, "Earth Facing 'Catastrophic' Loss of Species," *Guardian*, July 20, 2006. Tim Radford, "Two-Thirds of World's Resources 'Used Up,'" (reporting on the UN Milennium Eco Assessment), *Guardian*, March 30, 2005; Geoffrey Lean, "Disaster Warning from UN as Investigation Reveals Half the Planet's 500 Biggest Rivers Are Seriously Depleted or Polluted," *Independent*, March 12, 2006; Alex Kirby, "Extinction Nears for Whales and Dolphins," BBC News Online, May 14, 2003. Richard Black, "Only 50 Years Left' for Sea Fish," BBC News Online, November 2, 2006. And on and on.

Beckett, eliciting howls of protest.[8] For all Blair's hypocrisy, EU leaders were no better. The European Union, "self-styled global champion in the battle against climate change, is falling woefully short of its targets for cutting greenhouse gas emissions and will need to take radical measures to achieve them," the *Independent* reported in 2005.[9]

So why is it that at every turn, seemingly sincere political leaders find that even with the best of intentions, and after all their promises, they can't bring themselves to subordinate growth to protecting the planet, and instead turn themselves into hypocrites and liars, and doom the future for their own children?

I. The Smithian operating system

To understand why capitalism and the market can't solve our global environmental crisis, the place to start is with an examination of the logic and contradictions of capitalist economics, which is to say, the economics of Adam Smith. Obviously, Smith can't be held responsible for the problems and consequences of capitalist development in our day. But Smith's economic theory is a metonym, what we might call the intellectual operating system of capitalism. For it was Smith, the original and foremost theorist of capitalism, who first discovered and elaborated the organizing principle of capitalist economic life, which he famously termed the "invisible hand". Smith found it a remarkable fact that in what he called "commercial society" (what we today call capitalism), no one knows what or how much in the way of provisions, the necessities of life – food, enough clothes, housing, transportation and so on – society actually wants from day to day, year to year, generation to generation. Yet somehow this seems to get *more or less* taken

---

[8] Geoffrey Lean, "Scrap UK Pollution Targets, Says Brown," *Independent*, November 6, 2005; Geoffrey Lean, "Blair Blocked Plan to Cut Emissions," *Independent*, April 2, 2006; Amanda Brown, "Howard Attacks Labour over Climate Change," *Independent*, September 13, 2004.

[9] Barrie Clement, "Europeans Missing Their Kyoto Targets," *Independent*, December 27, 2005. Keith Bradsher, "Emissions by China Accelerate Rapidly," *New York* Times, November 7, 2006. David Gow, "Europe Falls Far Short of Kyoto Targets," *Guardian Weekly*, November 3–9, 2006; BBC, "Climate Change: The Big Emitters," July 4, 2005: http://news.bbc.co.uk/2/hi/science/nature/3143798.stm. International Energy Outlook 2006, www.eia.doe.gov/oiaf/ieo/emissions.html. Marie Woolf, "G8 Will Not Set Targets to Cut Global Warming," *Independent*, May 28, 2005.

care of – unconsciously, without any plan. In some of the most famous phrases in all of economic literature Smith asserted that:

> "In almost every other race of animals each individual, when it grows up to maturity, is entirely independent, and in its natural state has occasion for the assistance of no other living creature. But man has almost constant occasion for the help of his brethren, and it is in vain for him to expect it from their benevolence only. He will be more likely to prevail if he can interest their self-love in his favour, and shew them that it is for their own advantage to do for him what he requires of them. Whoever offers to another a bargain of any kind, proposes to do this. Give me that which I want, and you shall have this which you want... and it is in this manner that we obtain from one another the far greater part of those good offices which we stand in need of. It is not from the benevolence of the butcher, the brewer, or the baker, that we expect our dinner, but from their regard to their own interest. We address ourselves, not to their humanity but to their self-love, and never talk to them of our own necessities but of their advantages" (book 1, chapter 1, p. 14).

But Smith drew this out beyond the mere commercial provisioning of commodities, of goods and services, to establish a broader point about the market and "public interest" – the common good of society as a whole. Thus he claimed that the best means of assuring the common good of society was to ignore it, not try to consciously, deliberately, and collectively act outside the market to benefit the common good. He argued that by pursuing our individual "self interest" and "self-love" the common good would be taken care of by the "invisible hand" of the market. He could say this because, in his view, the public interest of society was no more than the sum of its private interests:

> "Every individual... neither intends to promote the public interest, nor knows how much he is promoting it... He intends only his own gain, and he is in this, as in many other cases, led by an invisible hand to promote an end which was no part of his intention. Nor is it always the worse for the society that it was no part of it. By pursuing his own interest he frequently promotes that of the

society more effectually than when he really intends to promote it. I have never known much good done by those who affected to trade for the public good. It is an affectation, indeed, not very common among merchants, and very few words need be employed in dissuading them from it" (book 4, chapter 2, p. 423).[10]

This broader argument about the public interest is deeply problematic, and I'll come back to it below. But Smith's theorization of the invisible hand as economic organizer of "commercial society" is one of the most powerful and elegant concepts of all capitalist economics. It grasped the essence of the market system – namely, production for exchange, specialized division of labor and mutual dependence of all producers / commodity sellers / consumers upon one another through the market. This is indeed what distinguishes the market system from all previous economic systems such as communal tribal society, slavery, feudalism – all of which were in one way or another systems based exclusively, or for the most part, on direct production for use rather than for exchange.

So for example, in medieval agrarian Europe, farm production was planned production and largely for direct use. The basic unit of rural production was the peasant family with its farm, its rudimentary tools, and its livestock. Peasant farmers not only grew their own food but often made their own clothes, fabricated most of their own tools, built their own houses, and so on. Peasants produced mostly for subsistence and, where they were enserfed, to pay rents to feudal landlords, tithes to the church and, sometimes, additional obligations to the state. Beyond this, those who could produce and retain some surplus over subsistence and rent and tithe obligations, sold it in local town markets to procure the few necessities they could not produce for themselves on the farm or the lord's demesne shops – metal for plows or tools and such. In the villages, patriarchal family households organized the day-to-day operations of farm life, determining which crops to grow and when, and assigning a division of labor within the family. They planned this production based on their foreknowledge of what their family unit needed to carry on from year to year – how much and what kinds of crops and animals to raise, how much labor to devote to farming, husbandry, building upkeep, and so on. More often than not, because village agricultural regimes required village-wide cooperation to regulate seasonal plantings, field rotations, harvest, commons management, and so on,

---

[10] *An Inquiry into the Nature and Causes of the Wealth of Nations* (New York: The Modern Library, 1965).

peasant farmers collectively planned and regulated their seasonal work rhythms in cooperation with their neighbors according to custom and village bylaws in tight-knit village communities. Throughout Europe, most rural agrarian output was directly consumed on the farm and in the hamlets and villages. The feudal aristocracy consumed the surpluses directly and marketed some of their surpluses in urban markets to purchase luxury goods and military equipment. In short, rural Europe, at least up to the 15th century, was in a sense a "planned" economy – or more precisely, Europe was comprised in the main of masses of miniature planned village economies.[11]

By Adam Smith's day in the late 18th century, rural peasant village self-sufficiency, with its limited division of labor and limited productivity, had largely given way to generalized production for market throughout England and over much of Western Europe. In this new "commercial" economy, there was no general economic "plan". No one was self-sufficient anymore. Production was no longer for direct consumption by the family. Production was increasingly geared to sell to the whole society – and it was to others, to society, that one had to turn to satisfy one's own necessary wants, as Smith noted. In this system, unlike the feudal peasant village, no one knew how much or what kinds of crops society needed, how many shoes or coats society needed, how many houses or ships or wagons needed to be built, or when, and so on. No one consciously divided up and assigned society's labor to the various tasks of producing all that society required.[12] No one knew how much of these things society needed in any given year. Indeed, no one even cared. And yet despite, or rather because of, the "mindlessness" of this system, instead of the chaos one might expect, there emerged a kind of spontaneous order. Society seems to be "guided by an invisible hand" to produce more or less enough of these goods that we carry on from day to day, to ensure social reproduction. So how does this "miracle" of the "invisible hand" happen?

[11] Warren O. Ault, *Open-Field Farming in Medieval England* (London: George Allen & Unwin, 1972); Alan Mayhew, *Rural Settlement and Farming in Germany* (New York: Barnes & Noble, 1973); B. H. Slicher Van Bath, *The Agrarian History of Western Europe A.D. 500–1850* (London: Edward Arnold, 1963); Jack Goody et al., *Family and Inheritance: Rural Society in Western Europe 1200–1800* (Cambridge: Cambridge University Press, 1976).
[12] "This division of labour, from which so many advantages are derived, is not originally the effect of any human wisdom, which foresees and intends that general opulence to which it gives occasion. It is the necessary, though very slow and gradual, consequence of a certain propensity in human nature . . . the propensity to truck, barter, and exchange one thing for another." Smith, *Wealth of Nations*, book I, chap. II, p. 13.

How did the common good become a bad idea?

The invisible hand is of course the market. In the developing 18th-century capitalist economy of Adam Smith's era, most producers no longer possessed their own means of subsistence – or at least full subsistence. Masses of peasant farmers had been cleared off the land and proletarianized by centuries of enclosure movements. Peasant subsistence farms, with all their variety of produce, had been extensively replaced with monocrop regimes of wheat farms or sheepfolds. The hand-loom weaver, the village blacksmith, and most such small-scale, hand manufactures were giving way to large-scale factory production with a specialized division of labor and, increasingly in the late 18th century, mechanization. In result, the factory owner, millworker, farmer, mechanic, clerk, doctor, lawyer – no one in commodity society grew his/her own food, made his/her own tools, his/her own clothes, and so on, as once their ancestors had done. Because we lack full access to the means of subsistence, everyone in capitalist society must specialize to produce a commodity for market or sell their labor power to work for an employer who does possess the means of production.[13] So to win one's own bread in the capitalist organization of production, virtually everyone, including the capitalists, must sell their specialized commodity on the market in order to purchase their own means of subsistence and to purchase the means of production to re-enter production, and on it goes.[14] In this way each and every commodity producer/seller is *dependent* upon the labor of others.[15]

---

[13] "It is the maxim of every prudent master of a family, never to attempt to make at home what it will cost him more to make than to buy. The tailor does not attempt to make his own shoes, but buys them of the shoemaker. The shoemaker does not attempt to make his own clothes but employs a tailor. The farmer attempts to make neither the one nor the other, but employs those different artificers. All of them find it for their interest to employ their whole industry in a way in which they have some advantage over their neighbors, and to purchase with a part of its produce, or what is the same thing, with the price of part of it, whatever else they have occasion for." *Ibid.*, book I, chap. II, *op cit.* p. 15.

[14] "When the division of labour has been once thoroughly established, it is but a very small part of a man's wants which the produce of his labour can supply. He supplies the far greater part of them by exchanging that surplus part of the produce of his won labour, which is over and above his own consumption, for such parts of the produce of other men's labour as he has occasion for. Every man thus lives by exchanging, or becomes in some measure a merchant, and the society itself grows to be what is properly a commercial society." *Ibid.*, book I, chap. IV, *op cit.* p. 22.

[15] So after his famous discussion of the division of labor in the modern pin-making factory of the eighteenth century, with its eighteen or so specialized occupations, Smith says, "In every other art and manufacture, the effects of the division of labour are similar to what they are in this very trifling one . . . How many different trades are employed in each branch of the linen and woollen manufactures, from the growers of the flax and the wool, to the bleachers and smoothers of the linen, or to the dyers and dressers of the cloth!" *Ibid.*, book I, chap. I, *op. cit.* pp. 5–6.

How do these specialist commodity producers/sellers know how much of their particular commodity – wheat, cloth, bricks, horseshoes, board feet of lumber, barrels, and so on to bring to market, how much can they likely expect to sell in a given week or year? They don't. No one knows in advance. Everyone estimates in advance of going to market, often based on how much they sold the previous year, and brings their product to market hoping to sell it for at least as high a price as other producer/sellers of the same commodity. Society's "need" for any particular commodity is determined after the fact by the price at which it sells – what Smith called "effectual demand". If demand and prices are high for some commodity, Smith says producers will "employ more labour and stock in preparing and bringing it to market". If demand falls, producers will "withdraw a part of their labour or stock from this employment" and redeploy those resources in some other line of production.[16] So if the market is glutted with wheat, but wool is in short supply and prices are high, some farmers will turn to sheep-raising. If demand is low for ships but high for houses, some carpenters will move out of ship-building and into house-building. And so on, until the supply and demand of society's commodities are roughly in balance – what economists today call "equilibrium."[17] So: no plan. The market shows us what society "needs" through the movement of prices. That's the beauty and efficiency of the market system – as mainstream economists never tire of telling us.

---

[16] "The market price of every particular commodity is regulated by the proportion between the quantity which is actually brought to market, and the demand of those who are willing to pay the natural price of the commodity... Such people may be called the effectual demanders, and their demand the effectual demand; since it may be sufficient to effectuate the bringing of the commodity to market... When the quantity of any commodity which is brought to market falls short of the effectual demand... the market price will rise... When the quantity brought to market exceeds the effectual demand... the market price will sink... (and this will prompt employers) to withdraw a part of their labour or stock from this employment." Here Smith doesn't actually follow his own line of thought to its logical conclusion: He says that sinking prices will compel employers to withdraw labor and resources from employment in a given line of production, but he does not say that the employer (as investor) will then need to reemploy those assets elsewhere, in some *other* line of production, which may or may not be practicable for the particular employer. But that conclusion nevertheless follows from his logic and such capital mobility is in fact the actual practice of investors. *Ibid., op cit.* book I, chapter VII, op cit. pp. 56–57.

[17] "When the quantity brought to market is just sufficient to supply the effectual demand and no more... the whole quantity upon hand can be disposed of for this price, and cannot be disposed of for more. The competition of the different dealers obliges them all to accept of this price... It is in the interest of all those who employ their land, labour, or stock, in bringing any commodity to market, that the quantity never should exceed the effectual demand; and it is in the interest of all other people that it never should fall short of demand." *Ibid.,* book I, chap. VII, p. 57.

II. Engine of development: production for exchange and its imperatives

This circumstance of mutual dependence of each and every person through the market entrains a number of powerful implications. Foremost among these are the implications that flow from *competition* in the marketplace. Commodity sellers don't have the freedom to charge what they wish because when they come to market they face other producers selling the same commodity. To compete, producers must be able to sell at prices close to the competition, and therefore must produce their commodity at least as cheaply as other producers. So producers are compelled to adopt specific strategies and methods to survive against competition and these shape the overall pattern of economic development of capitalism as a system and also distinguish this system from every other economic system.

First, producers must strive to *cut the cost of inputs* – to seek out ever-cheaper sources of raw materials and cheaper labor. Producers are compelled to *increase the efficiency* of their units of production by innovating, by bringing in more advanced labor-saving machinery to boost productivity, by substituting newer and cheaper raw material inputs, to systematically introduce efficiencies in every aspect of production. This means that unlike the ruling classes of pre-capitalist economies, capitalists are not free to consume their surpluses in conspicuous consumption but are compelled to *reinvest much of their profits* back into productivity-enhancing technologies and skills, to *develop the forces of production* and with these, the whole economy, in order to compete. Competition compels producers *to strive to grow*, to maximize sales, to expand existing markets, to *seek out new markets, to create new markets*, create new commodities – or see them developed by the competition, and thus see their stock value fall as the penalty for complacency. There can be no stasis, no rest, no complacency. Eloquent as Adam Smith was, no one captured the broader developmental implications of capitalist economics better than Karl Marx. In some of the most prescient and eloquent phrases in all of economic literature Marx wrote in his and Engels's *Communist Manifesto* that:

> "The bourgeoisie cannot exist without constantly revolutionising the instruments of production, and thereby the relations of production, and with them the whole relations of society... Constant revolutionising of production, uninterrupted disturbance of all social conditions, everlasting uncertainty and agitation distinguish the bourgeois epoch from all earlier ones. All fixed,

15

fast-frozen relations, with their train of ancient and venerable prejudices and opinions, are swept away, all new-formed ones become antiquated before they can ossify. All that is solid melts into air, all that is holy is profaned...

"The need of a constantly expanding market for its products chases the bourgeoisie over the entire surface of the globe. It must nestle everywhere, settle everywhere, establish connexions everywhere.

"The bourgeoisie has through its exploitation of the world market given a cosmopolitan character to production and consumption in every country... All old-established national industries have been destroyed or are daily being destroyed. They are dislodged by new industries... that no longer work up indigenous raw material, but raw material drawn from the remotest zones; industries whose products are consumed, not only at home, but in every quarter of the globe. In place of the old wants, satisfied by the production of the country, we find new wants, requiring for their satisfaction the products of distant lands and climes. In place of the old local and national seclusion and self-sufficiency, we have intercourse in every direction, universal inter-dependence of nations...

"The bourgeoisie, by the rapid improvement of all instruments of production, by the immensely facilitated means of communication, draws all, even the most barbarian, nations into civilisation. The cheap prices of commodities are the heavy artillery with which it batters down all Chinese walls, with which it forces the barbarians' intensely obstinate hatred of foreigners to capitulate. It compels all nations, on pain of extinction, to adopt the bourgeois mode of production; it compels them to introduce what it calls civilisation into their midst, i.e., to become bourgeois themselves. In one word, it creates a world after its own image...

"The bourgeoisie, during its rule of scarce one hundred years, has created more massive and more colossal productive forces than have all preceding generations together. Subjection of Nature's

> forces to man, machinery, application of chemistry to industry and agriculture, steam-navigation, railways, electric telegraphs, clearing of whole continents for cultivation, canalisation or rivers, whole populations conjured out of the ground—what earlier century had even a presentiment that such productive forces slumbered in the lap of social labour?"[18]

By comparison, pre-capitalist modes of production contained no such engine of development, no such drive to "constantly revolutionize" the instruments and relations of production. Technological advance under slavery, under feudalism and so on was agonizingly slow, and economic stagnation was the norm, with the inevitable result that productivity frequently could not keep pace with population growth. And so economic collapse and famine followed as regular features of these economic systems. Even the Stalinist bureaucratic mode of production in Russia, China and other countries contained no such inherent drive to development. Post-revolutionary Russia and China did develop and industrialize to a considerable extent and rapidly. But the impetus to that development was not built into the organization of production itself. The impetus depended entirely on the conscious actions and direction of central planners, but for the same reason, it was also severely limited and handicapped by the bureaucracy's inability to push development beyond certain limits, to use the weapon of unemployment and firm bankruptcy to discipline producers, to force productivity increases, and to generate innovation and development – as under capitalism.[19] Because that system contained no built-in drive, no pressure of competition to force producers to innovate, to bring in efficiencies and so on, in the end, top-down, bureaucratically driven development was no match for the dynamic and inexorable growth of global capitalism.

This built-in engine of development has brought the most prodigious development of the forces of production of any mode of production in history, lifting the living standards of billions of people the world over. So it was no surprise that with the spectacular collapse of communism and the global triumph of capitalism in the

---

[18] *Marx & Engels: Basic Writings on Politics and Philosophy*, Lewis S. Feuer, ed. (New York: Doubleday, 1959), pp. 10–12.

[19] I explored some of the internal economic dynamics of the Stalinist-type bureaucratic mode of production in my PhD thesis "Class Structure and Economic Development: The Contradictions of Market Socialism in China," UCLA, Department of History, 1989. And I published some of this analysis in "The Chinese Road to Capitalism," *New Left Review* 199 (May–June 1993).

1990s, Smithian economics has been crowned with a sacred halo, unquestioned and self-evident to the churched.[20] Smith's theory, retailed for today's market under the neoclassical and neoliberal labels, is entrenched in every economics department from Berkeley to Beijing.

III. Engine of planetary eco-collapse: the collective irrationality of individualist economics

The problem is that while capitalism has brought unprecedented development, this same motor of development is now driving towards ecological collapse, threatening to doom us all. And Smithian capitalist economics can offer no solution to the crisis because the crisis is the product of the same dynamic of competition-driven production for market that generates the ever-greater accumulation of wealth and consumption that Smithian economists celebrate. In his 1996 book *The Future of Capitalism*, Lester Thurow lucidly captured the socially suicidal aggregate impact of individualistic economic decision-making:

> "Nowhere is capitalism's time horizon problem more acute than in
> the area of global environmentalism... What should a capitalistic
> society do about long-run environmental problems such as global
> warming or ozone depletion?... Using capitalist decision rules, the
> answer to what should be done today to prevent such problems is
> very clear—do nothing. However large the negative effects fifty to
> one hundred years from now might be, their current discounted net
> present value is zero. If the current value of the future negative
> consequences is zero, then nothing should be spent today to
> prevent those distant problems from emerging. But if the negative
> effects are very large fifty to one hundred years from now, by then
> it will be too late to do anything to make the situation any better,
> since anything done at that time could only improve the situation

---

[20] As Gary Becker the Nobel Prize winning Chicago economist trumpeted in the nineties: "The collapse of communism is the most significant political and economic event of the past half century. It is unassailable proof that capitalism with free markets is the most effective system yet devised for raising both economic well-being and political freedom. 'Chicago' economics argued this for many decades, but it took the dramatic end of communism to show that what is true in theory and in the past also holds in the modern world." Gary S. Becker and Guity Nashat Becker, *The Economics of Life* (New York: McGraw-Hill, 1997), p. 241.

another fifty to one hundred years into the future. So being good capitalists, those who live in the future, no matter how bad their problems are, will also decide to do nothing. Eventually a generation will arrive which cannot survive in the earth's altered environment, but by then it will be too late for them to do anything to prevent their own extinction. Each generation makes good capitalist decisions, yet the net effect is collective social suicide."[21]

Lester Thurow, almost alone among mainstream economists as near as I can tell, recognizes this potentially fatal contradiction of capitalism – even though he is no anti-capitalist and wrote the book from which this excerpt is drawn in the hopes of finding a future *for* capitalism. Until very recently the standard economics textbooks ignored the problem of the environment altogether. Even today, the standard Econ 101 textbooks of Barro, Mankiv and so on, contain almost no mention of environment or ecology and virtually no serious consideration of the problem.[22] This reflects the increasingly rightward drift of the discipline since the seventies. The American economics profession has long-since abandoned the practice of critical

---

[21] Lester Thurow, *The Future of Capitalism* (New York: Penguin Books, 1996), pp. 302–3.

[22] Given the gravity of the issue, and given that economic development is the driving engine of ecological destruction, it might seem surprising that most economists have little or nothing say about the environment and its relation to the economy. But a survey of introductory macroeconomic textbooks used by most US economics departments is revealing of the profession's lack of contact with reality. Perhaps one might not expect Paul Samuelson's *Economics*, long the classic text in the field, to deal with the environment. It was written in 1948. But recent editions offer no improvement in this regard. Robert J. Barro, author of a widely used new text *Macroeconomics* (MIT, 1997), and *cause célèbre* as the most sought after and highest paid professor of economics in the country, makes no mention of the environment or pollution in 867 pages of text. Same with Stephen J. Turnovsky, Castor Professor of Economics at the University of Washington, another high-flying economist and author of *International Macroeconomic Dynamics* (MIT, 1997). No mention either in *Foundations of Economic Analysis* (Harvard UP, Enlarged edition 1983) by Maurice Obstfeld of Berkeley and Kenneth Rogoff of Princeton. With a title like *The Age of Diminished Expectations* (MIT, 1994) one might expect that Paul Krugman, then Ford Professor of Economics at MIT, emphatic liberal, and widely hailed as "the most celebrated economist of his generation" would mention the environment. No mention. Krugman's introductory economics textbook, *Macroeconomics* (Worth Publishers, 2005) written with Robin Wells, does actually devote a few pages (6 out of 897) to the environment. But this is entirely focused on pricing environmental "externatlities," proffering the usual tried-and-failed market-based "win-win" panaceas that have had such little positive effect so far, and shows no awareness of the problem of the inherently fatal logic of capitalist development that Thurow raised back in 1996.

scientific thought to seriously dissenting views. Today, a neo-totalitarian "neoliberal" religious dogma rules the discipline. Keynesianism, liberalism, to say nothing of Marxism, are all dismissed as hopelessly antiquated, ecological economics is suspect, and the prudent graduate student would be well advised to steer clear of such interests if he or she wants to find a job.[23] As Francis Fukuyama put it back in the 90s after communism collapsed, history has reached its penultimate apogee in free-market capitalism and liberal democracy. The science of economics, Fukuyama pronounced, was "settled" with Adam Smith's accomplishment. The future would bring no more than "endless technical adjustments" and no further theoretical thought is required or need be solicited.[24]

---

[23] Numerous experiments, polls, and critical studies have shown that the economics profession tends to recruit students who have already developed an inordinately self-interested, selfish, antisocial predisposition. This fits perfectly with the mainstream "business school" orientation of the profession, which has elevated the ideology of self-interestedness and methodological individualism to the level of a first principle and moral axiom. Experiments and polls showed that, generally speaking, entering economics graduate students tend to eschew contributing to society or the community, they find the concept of "fairness" alien. And once inducted into the guild, the profession brings to bear a powerful array of forces to correctly socialize the economist-in-training. Students' interests are systematically narrowed. They find that relations with professors and fellow students (future colleagues) are made more comfortable by hewing to a wide range of commonly shared assumptions and values, which are taken as self-evident and in no need of critical analysis. New generations build on the work of earlier ones without ever questioning its relevance, or, as Milton Friedman penned in his dedication of Capitalism and Freedom to the next generation, "carry on the torch of liberty on its next lap". The effort is always and only to fit new realities such as appear (for example, environmental pollution) into the old model (as "externalities" to be managed by some market-fix someday). The imprudent student who deigns to question the dominant view, the received wisdom of the elders, finds jobs scarce. Editors turn down their articles and books for publication. They find themselves marginalized or driven out of the profession by denial of tenure. So ideologically totalitarian is the profession that, in a critical letter to the journal Science, the economist Vassily Leontief remarked that the methods employed to maintain intellectual discipline within the academic discipline of economics can, he says, "occasionally remind one of those employed by the Marines to maintain discipline on Parris Island." See Herman Daly and John Cobb, *For the Common Good: Redirecting the Economy toward Community, the Environment, and a Sustainable Future* (Boston: Beacon Press, 1989), pp. 34–35 and pp. 90–91; D. Collander and A. Klamer, "The Making of an Economist," *Economic Perspectives* 1 (1987) pp. 95–111; Steven E. Rhoads, *The Economist's View of the World* (Cambridge: Cambridge University Press, 1985), pp. 161–62; and Wassily Leontief, letter to the editor, *Science* 217 (July 9, 1982) pp. 104–5. See also, Edward S. Herman, *Triumph of the Market* (Boston: South End Press, 1995) chapter 5, and Louis Uchitelle, "Students Are Leaving the Politics Out of Economics," *New York Times*, January 27, 2006.

[24] Francis Fukuyama, *The End of History and the Last Man* (New York: Free Press, 1992).

How did the common good become a bad idea?

Economic theology and denial: free-market economists versus the fact of limits

For Smithian economists, the notion that there are, or should be, limits to economic growth is just beyond the pale of thinkable thought. For to admit that growth is *a* problem, let alone *the* problem, is to concede a fatal flaw in the whole system and opens the door to challenge from the left. So across the entire spectrum of mainstream economics, Smithian economists, for all their important differences, still all belong to the same church of "Can't Stop Shopping" and worship the same idols of growth and consumption. At the extreme right, market fundamentalists like Milton Friedman, Gary Becker and adherents of the Chicago school simply deny that there *is* any environmental problem, certainly none that the market can't solve. Thus, in a 1991 interview, Milton Friedman ridiculed environmentalists with his trademark condescending and nasty vitriol:

> "The environmental movement consists of two very different parts. One is the traditional conservation groups, who want to save resources et cetera. The other is a group of people who fundamentally aren't interested in conservation at all, and who aren't primarily interested in pollution. They're just long-term anti-capitalists who will take every opportunity to trash the capitalist system and the market economy. They used to be communists or socialists, but history has been unkind to them, and now all they can do is complain about pollution. But without modern technology, pollution would be far worse. The pollution from horses was much worse than what you get from automobiles. If you read descriptions of the streets of New York in the nineteenth century..."[25]

And in his sadoeconomic screed *Free to Choose*, the anti-communist warhorse complained that:

> "...whatever the announced objectives, all of the movements of the past two decades—the consumer movement, the ecology movement, the back-to-the-land movement, the hippie movement, the organic food movement, the protect-the-wilderness movement,

---

[25] Quoted in Carla Ravaioli, *Economists and the Environment* (London: Zed Books, 1995), p. 11.

the zero-population-growth movement, the 'small is beautiful' movement, the antinuclear movement—have always had one thing in common. All have been antigrowth. They have been opposed to new developments, to industrial innovation, to the increased use of natural resources. Agencies established in response to these movements have imposed heavy costs on industry after industry..." [and so on].[26]

Friedman's redneck eco-know-nothingism has long defined the far-right wing of US economic theology but his confident assumption that endless growth is sustainable is shared by the entire profession of mainstream economists regardless of their important differences. If we look at the far-left extreme of acceptable economic thought, say Paul Krugman, we hear the same "can't stop progress" mantra: writing in the *New York Times* Krugman wonders "if there isn't something a bit manic about the pace of getting and – especially – spending in *fin-de-siècle* America":

"But there is one very powerful argument that can be made on behalf of recent American consumerism: not that it is good for consumers, but that it has been good for producers. You see, spending may not produce happiness, but it does create jobs, and unemployment is very effective at creating misery. Better to have manic consumers American style, than the depressive consumers of Japan... There is a strong element of rat race in America's consumer-led boom, but those rats racing in their cages are what keep the wheels of commerce turning. And while it will be a shame if Americans continue to compete over who can own the most toys, the worst thing of all would be if the competition comes to a sudden halt."[27]

Paul Krugman is a brilliant economist but the Smithian premises of his theoretical framework cannot allow that we could actually run out of resources to make all those toys.

---

[26] Milton Friedman and Rose Friedman, *Free to Choose* (New York: Harcourt Brace Janovich, 1990), p. 191.
[27] "Money Can't Buy Happiness. Er, Can It?," op-ed, *New York Times*, June 1, 1999.

How did the common good become a bad idea?

There you have it: insatiable growth and consumption are destroying the planet and will doom humanity in the long run – but without ceaselessly growing production and insatiably rising consumption, we would have economic collapse in the short run.

Who looks out for common good?

Adam Smith's economics is an idea whose time has passed. Specialization, planless, anarchic production for market, single-minded pursuit of profit maximization at the expense of all other considerations, was the driving engine that generated the greatest advances in industrial and agricultural productivity, and also the greatest accumulation of wealth the world has ever seen. But that same engine of development, now immensely larger and running at full throttle, is overdeveloping the world economy, overconsuming the world's resources, flooding the world's waters and atmosphere with toxic and warming pollution, and propelling us off the cliff to ecological collapse, if not extinction. Adam Smith's fatal error – fatal for *us* – was his assumption that the "most effectual" means of promoting the public interest, the common good of society, is to just ignore it and focus exclusively on the pursuit of individual economic self-interest.

Even with respect to the public interest of the economic welfare of society, Smith's thesis that the invisible hand of the market would *automatically* bring about "universal opulence which extends itself to the lowest ranks of the people" as "a general plenty diffuses itself through all the different ranks of the society" could hardly have been more mistaken. Two-and-a-quarter centuries after Smith wrote, global capitalist development has produced the most obscenely unequal societies in history, with half the world living on less than two dollars a day, billions of people living in desperate poverty, many times more than the entire population of the world in Smith's day, while a tiny global elite, even just a few hundred individuals, concentrate an ever-growing share of the world's wealth, which they lavish on "opulence" on a hitherto unimagined scale. On this breath-taking failure of social scientific prediction alone, Smith's economic theory ought to have been ridiculed and drummed out of the profession long ago, as such a comparable predictive failure would have been in the natural sciences.

With respect to the public interest of broader societal concerns, which today would include the environment, Smith's philosophy of economic individualism as the

23

means to maximize the public interest – the common good of society – is not only completely wrongheaded, it's suicidal. And it is completely at odds with the world's scientists and scientific bodies who are crying out for a *plan* – a plan to stop global warming, to save the forests, to save the fisheries, to stop ocean acidification, to detoxify the planet, to save the thousands of creatures from extinction, etc.[28] But capitalist economists, even the most humane like Paul Krugman or Joe Stiglitz, are hostile to the idea of economic planning.

Corporations aren't necessarily evil. They just can't help themselves. The problem is that the critical decisions that affect the environment, decisions about what and how much to produce, about resource consumption, about pollution – are not in society's hands and not even in the hands of the government. Those decisions are in private hands, mainly in the hands of large corporations. Thus when these imperatives clash, CEOs have no choice but to make systematically wrong decisions. In Adam Smith's day this didn't matter so much because companies were so small and had little impact on the environment. But today, when huge corporations have the power, the technology and every incentive to melt the icecaps, it matters. Leaving the global economy in the hands of private corporations, subject to the demands of the market, is the road to collective eco-suicide.

---

[28] At a "floating symposium" organized by the Massachusetts-based Woods Hole Research Institute on the Rio Negro in July 2006, top international scientists warned that "global warming and deforestation were rapidly pushing the entire enormous area towards a 'tipping point' where it would irreversibly start to die. The consequences would be truly awesome. The wet Amazon, the planet's greatest celebration of life, would turn to dry savannah at best, desert at worst. This would cause much of the world – including Europe – to become hotter and drier, making this sweltering summer a mild foretaste of what is to come. In the longer term, it could make global warming spiral out of control, eventually making the world uninhabitable... If we do not act now [said one scientist] we will lose the Amazon forest that helps sustain living conditions throughout the world." Geoffrey Lean, "Dying forest: one year to save the Amazon" *The Independent*, July 23, 2006. Also, Geoffrey Lean and Fred Pearce, "Amazon rainforest 'could become a desert,'" *The Independent*, July 23, 2006.Also: David Adam, "Time running out to curb effects of deep sea pollution," *The Guardian*, June 17, 2006. Tim Radford, "Scientists call for urgent action to save Atlantic tuna," *The Guardian*, April 28, 2005. Steve Connor, "Scientists condemn US as emission of greenhouse gases hit record level," *The Independent*, April 19, 2006. Ian Sample, "Earth facing 'catastrophic loss of species'", *The Guardian*, July 20, 2006

ESSAY 2 (2010)

Beyond growth or beyond capitalism?

Abstract: Recent publications have revived interest in Herman Daly's proposal for a Steady- State Economy. This paper argues, first, that the idea of a steady-state capitalism is based on untenable assumptions, starting with the assumption that growth is optional rather than built- into capitalism. I argue that irresistible and relentless pressures for growth are functions of the day-to-day requirements of capitalist reproduction in a competitive market, incumbent upon all but a few businesses, and that such pressures would prevail in any conceivable capitalism. Secondly, this paper takes issue with Professor Daly's thesis, which also underpins his SSE model, that capitalist efficiency and resource allocation is the best we can come up with. I argue that this belief is misplaced and incompatible with an ecological economy, and therefore it undermines Daly's own environmental goals. I conclude that since capitalist growth cannot be stopped, or even slowed, and since the market-driven growth is driving us toward collapse, ecological economists should abandon the fantasy of a steady-state capitalism and get on with the project figuring out what a post–capitalist economic democracy could look like.

Under the headline "Economic Growth 'Cannot Continue'" the BBC on January 28, 2010 summarized a report issued by the New Economics Foundation (NEF) which asserts that "continuing economic growth is not possible if nations are to tackle climate change". The NEF says that "unprecedented and probably impossible" carbon reductions would be needed to hold temperature rises below 2°C (3.6°F) without which we face catastrophic global warming. "We urgently need to change our economy to live within its environmental budget," said NEF's policy director Andrew Simms, adding that, "There is no global, environmental central bank to bail us out if we become ecologically bankrupt."[1] In *Growth Isn't Possible* Simms and

---

[1] New Economic Foundation, *Growth Isn't Possible*, January 25, 2010 (London NEF, 2010) at http://www.neweconomics.org/publications/growth-isnt-possible.

his co-author Victoria Johnson reviewed all the existing proposed models for dealing with climate change and energy use including renewable, carbon capture and storage, nuclear, and even geo-engineering, and concluded that these are "potentially dangerous distractions from more human-scale solutions" and that there are "no magic bullets" to save us. The report concludes that even if we were to rapidly transition to an entirely clean-energy based economy, this would not suffice to save us because: "Globally, we are consuming nature's services – using resources and creating carbon emissions – 44 percent faster than nature can regenerate and reabsorb what we consume and the waste we produce. In other words... if the whole world wished to consume at the same rate it would require 3.4 planets like Earth." Given these facts and trends, Simms and Johnson argue, we have no choice but to bring average global growth to a halt (with sharp reductions in growth in the industrialized countries balanced by accelerated growth in the developing countries to approximate equity but tend toward stasis on balance) and to radically reconstruct the global economy to conform to "environmental thresholds, which include biodiversity and the finite availability of natural resources." The authors conclude that "a new macro-economic model is needed, one that allows the human population as a whole to thrive without having to rely on ultimately impossible, endless increases in consumption" and they point to Herman Daly's idea of a "Steady-State Economy" as their model. For a reaction to this report, the BBC asked Tom Clougherty, executive director of the Adam Smith Institute, a free-market think tank, for his response. Clougherty remarked that the NEF's report exhibited "a complete lack of understanding of economics..."[2]

The NEF report came on the heels of a book published in December 2009 by Tim Jackson, Economics Commissioner on the Sustainable Development Commission, the UK government's independent advisor on sustainable development. In *Prosperity Without Growth* Jackson argues that our ever-increasing consumption adds little to human happiness, even impedes it, and is destroying our children's future. Jackson calls for a new vision of "prosperity without growth" and, like the NEF, points to Daly's Steady-State Economy as the best model.[3]

Now there is no doubt that the NEF is right that if CO_2 emissions continue to climb, catastrophic global warming will result. The NEF is also right that if there are no

---

[2] "Economic growth 'cannot continue'" BBCnews Online, January 25, 2010 at http://news.bbc.co.uk/2/hi/science/nature/8478770.stm.
[3] Tim Jackson, *Prosperity Without Growth* (London: Earthscan, 2009).

magic techno-fixes currently available, or in the foreseeable future, then the only way to stop global warming before it exceeds 2°C is to put the brakes on growth. But Tom Clougherty still had a point: pro-market but anti-growth economists don't understand capitalist economics. In rejecting the notion of a no-growth capitalism, Clougherty was just reaffirming the orthodox view of economists across the spectrum from Adam Smith to Karl Marx – that growth is an iron law of capitalist development, that capitalism cannot exist without constant revolutionizing of productive forces, without constantly expanding markets, without ever-growing consumption of resources.[4] Indeed, it was precisely this market-propelled "motor" of economic development that for Karl Marx so sharply distinguished the capitalist mode of production from all previous historical modes of production like slavery or feudalism, which contained no such in-built motor of development and so suffered repeatedly from stagnation, crises of *underproduction*, famine and collapse.[5] But of course *pace* the New Economics Foundation, the Adam Smith Institute believes that endless growth and ever-rising consumption are *good things*.

I. Why do capitalist economies grow?

Simms and Johnson begin by asking, "why do economies grow?" Their answer is that as a society we're "addicted" to growth.[6] Bill McKibben, in his Foreword to Tim Jackson's book calls growth a "spell": "For a couple of hundred years, economic growth really was enchanting." But "the endless growth of material economies" threatens the underpinnings of our civilization. The "spell" can be broken and it is past time we did it.[7] Jackson says we can find a sustainable prosperity if we abandon the growth-obsessed, resource-intensive consumer economy, forget "keeping up with the Joneses", and "live more meaningful lives" by "downshifting" to consume less, find "meaningful work" and "revitalize the notion

---

[4] Smith's theorization of growth was rudimentary but clear. He believed that "division of labor is limited by the extent of the market." As division of labor increases output and sales (increases "the extent of the market"), this induces the possibility of further division and labor and thus further growth. Thus, Smith argued, growth was self-reinforcing as it exhibited increasing returns to scale. Adam Smith, *The Wealth of Nations* (various editions) chaps 1 and 3.

[5] For a more detailed discussion of Smith and Marx on these points, see my "The eco-suicidal economics of Adam Smith," *Capitalism Nature Socialism* 18.2 9 (June 2007) pp. 22-43.

[6] *Growth Isn't Possible*, pp. 8-15.

[7] *Prosperity Without Growth*, pp. xiii-xiv.

of public goods". "People can flourish without more stuff" he says.[8] For Jackson, Simms and Johnson as for Daly, growth is seen to be entirely *subjective*, optional, not built into capitalist economies. So it can be dispensed with, exorcised, and capitalism can carry on in something like "stasis". So Tim Jackson tells us that in his vision of a "flourishing capitalism" the market would operate at a less frantic pace:

> "Ecological investment calls up a different 'investment ecology.' Capital productivity will probably fall. Returns will be lower and delivered over longer timeframes. Though vital for ecological integrity, some investments may not generate returns in conventional monetary terms. Profitability – in the traditional sense – will be diminished. In a growth-based economy, this is deeply problematic. For an economy concerned with flourishing it needn't matter at all."[9]

Reading this, it's not hard to see why mainstream economists find the idea of a slow growth, let alone a no-growth capitalism, hard to take seriously. For a start, *under capitalism*, this would just be a recipe for mass unemployment among many other problems. A decade ago in the midst of the boom, Paul Krugman, writing in *The New York Times* wondered "if there isn't something a bit manic about the pace of getting and – especially – spending in *fin-de-siècle* America":

> "But there is one very powerful argument that can be made on behalf of recent American consumerism: not that it is good for consumers, but that it has been good for producers. You see, spending may not produce happiness, but it does create jobs, and unemployment is very effective at creating misery. Better to have manic consumers American style, than depressive consumers of Japan... There is a strong element of rat race in America's consumer-led boom, but those rats racing in their cages are what keeps the wheels of commerce turning. And while it will be a shame if Americans continue to compete over who can own the

---

[8] *Ibid.*, pp. 132, 150-151, 171, 193.
[9] *Ibid.*, p. 197.

most toys, the worst thing of all would be if the competition comes
to a sudden halt."[10]

But then Paul Krugman is an economist. Ecological economists like to quote
Kenneth Boulding who famously declared that *"Anyone who believes exponential
growth can go on forever in a finite world is either a madman or an economist."*
Boulding, Daly and their students say that economists like Krugman are living in
denial if they think that growth can go on forever in a finite world. But Krugman
and the mainstream could just as easily reply that Boulding and Daly are *themselves*
living in denial if they think that capitalism can carry on without growing.

In what follows, I will argue that Herman Daly, Tim Jackson, Andrew Simms – and
the rest of the anti-growth school of ecological economists – are right: that we need
a new macro-economic model that allows us to thrive without endless consumption.
But they are wrong to think that this can be a capitalist economic model. I will try to
show why ecologically suicidal growth is built into the nature of *any conceivable
capitalism*. This means, I contend, that the project of a steady-state capitalism is
impossible and a distraction from what I think ought to the highest priority for
ecological economists today – which is to develop a broad conversation about what
the lineaments of a post-capitalist ecological economy could look like. I'm going to
start by stating three theses which I take to be fundamental principles and rules for
reproduction that define any capitalism, and shape the dynamics of capitalist
economic development:

1. Producers are dependent upon the market: Capitalism is a mode of production
in which specialized producers (corporations, companies, manufacturers, individual
producers) produce some commodity for market but do not produce their own means
of subsistence. Workers own no means of production, or insufficient means to enter
into production on their own, and so have no choice but to sell their labor to the
capitalists. Capitalists as a class possess a monopoly ownership of most of society's
means of production but do not directly produce their own means of subsistence. So
capitalists have to sell their commodities on the market to obtain money to buy their
own means of subsistence and to purchase new means of production and hire more

---

[10] "Money can't buy happiness. Er, can it?" *The New York Times*, June 1, 1999 Op-Ed. page.
Note to reader: I apologize for repeating this quotation which also appears in the previous
essay. As these two essays were previously published as articles and widely quoted,
sometimes citing this particular quotation, I opted not to revise them here.

labor, to re-enter production and carry on from year to year. So in a capitalist economy, everyone is dependent upon the market, compelled to sell in order to buy, to buy in order to sell to re-enter production and carry on.

2. Competition is the motor of economic development: When producers come to market they're not free to sell their particular commodity at whatever price they wish because they find other producers selling the same commodity. They therefore have to "meet or beat" the competition to sell their product and stay in business. Competition thus forces producers to *reinvest much of their profit* back into productivity-enhancing technologies and processes (instead of spending it on conspicuous consumption or warfare without developing the forces of production as ruling classes did, for example, under feudalism). Producers must constantly strive to *increase the efficiency* of their units of production by *cutting the cost of inputs,* seeking cheaper sources of raw materials and labor, by *bringing in more advanced labor-saving machinery and technology* to boost productivity, or by *increasing their scale of production* to take advantage of economies of scale, and in other ways, to *develop the forces of production.*

3. "Grow or die" is a law of survival in the marketplace: In the capitalist mode of production, most producers (there are some exceptions, which I will note below) have no choice but to live by the capitalist maxim "grow or die". First, as Adam Smith noted, the ever-increasing division of labor raises productivity and output, compelling producers to find more markets for this growing output. Secondly, competition compels producers to seek to expand their market share, to defend their position against competitors. Bigger is safer because, *ceteris paribus*, bigger producers can take advantage of economies of scale and can use their greater resources to invest in technological development, so can more effectively dominate markets. Marginal competitors tend to be crushed or bought out by larger firms (Chrysler, Volvo, etc.). Thirdly, the modern corporate form of ownership adds irresistible and unrelenting pressures to grow from owners (shareholders). Corporate CEOs do not have the freedom to choose not to grow or to subordinate profit-making to ecological concerns because they don't own their firms even if they own substantial shares. Corporations are owned by masses of shareholders. And the shareholders are not looking for "stasis"; they are looking to maximize portfolio gains, so they drive their CEOs forward.

Beyond growth or beyond capitalism?

In short, I maintain that the growth imperative is virtually a law of nature built-into in any conceivable capitalism. Corporations have no choice but to seek to grow. It is not "subjective". It is not just an "obsession" or a "spell". And it cannot be exorcised. Further, I maintain that these theses are uncontroversial, even completely obvious to mainstream economists across the ideological spectrum from Milton Friedman to Paul Krugman. But Herman Daly, Tim Jackson and the rest of the pro-market anti-growth school of ecological economists must *deny* these elementary capitalist rules for reproduction because their project for a "steady-state" eco-capitalism rests on the assumption that capitalist economic fundamentals are not immutable, that growth is "optional", and thus dispensable.

II. Ecological economics and the problem of growth

From the earliest efforts in the 1960s and 70s to bring ecological concerns to bear on capitalist economics and corporate practice beginning with the 1972 Club of Rome report *Limits to Growth*, mainstream pro-market eco-futurists, eco-capitalists and ecological economists have tried to deal with the problem of capitalist growth in one of two ways. Either, with Herman Daly and his school, who imagined that capitalism could be reconstructed such that it would more-or-less stop growing *quantitatively* but continue to *develop* internally – much as, Daly suggested, we ourselves stop growing physically at adolescence but continue to develop our capabilities, intellect, skills, etc. Or, with Paul Hawken, Lester Brown and other "sustainable development" proponents, they imagined that capitalism could carry on growing more-or-less forever, but that this growth could be rendered benign for the environment by forging an eco-entrepreneurial-led "green industrial revolution" and by introducing green subsidies and imposing carbon taxes, polluter pays penalties and the like, to bring the rest of industry on board. Pro-growth or anti-growth, both approaches assume that capitalism is sufficiently malleable that capitalist fundamentals can be "inverted" such that corporations can, in one way or another, be induced to subordinate profit-making to "saving the earth".[11] But what unites both schools of thought is their *a priori* rejection of alternatives to capitalism, their rejection of any kind of economic planning or socialism. So Jonathan Porrit, former Chairman of the UK Sustainable Development Commission, ex-Green Party Co-chair and one-time Director of Friends of the Earth, spoke for the mainstream when

---

[11] E.g. Hawken, *Ecological Commerce* (New York: HarperCollins, 1993) pp. 11-13.

he declared that, "Logically, whether we like it or not, sustainability is therefore going to have to be delivered within an all-encompassing capitalist framework. We don't have time to wait for any big-picture ideological successor."[12] I will address the problems of the pro-growth "sustainable capitalist" models of Paul Hawken et al. in separately. Here I am going to focus on the problems and contradictions of the pro-market, anti-growth school whose foremost theorist is Professor Herman Daly.

III. Capitalism without growth?

In the 1970s and 80s, Herman Daly launched a broadside assault on the academic discipline of economics assailing its dogmatic and neo-totalitarian embrace of neoclassical economics and its willful blindness to our looming environmental crisis. In ground-breaking and widely influential books and articles Daly assailed the "stupor of economic discourse" by holding up to his colleagues what he called the "wild facts" of our ecological crisis: the growing hole in the ozone shield, the alarming evidence of rising CO_2 levels, the shocking rates of natural resource consumption, the frightening rates of extinction and loss of biodiversity and so on, which mainstream economists ignored (and most continue to ignore to this day). The ecological crisis is caused, Daly argued, by too much growth: "the scale of human activity relative to the biosphere has grown too large" and most especially, by ever-growing consumption in the advanced industrialized countries. Daly attacked the mainstream's "idolatrous" "religion of growth," its "growthmania," its "fetish" of limitless consumption.[13] Daly's critique of the neoclassical defense of growth is probably the most devastating critique to come from within the profession.

But despite his "radical" break with the mainstream's fetish of growth, Daly did not at all break with his colleagues' fetish of the market organization of production, the capitalist market economy. On the contrary. His proposal for a Steady-State Economy was based, he said, "on impeccably respectable premises: private property, the free market, opposition to welfare bureaucracies and centralized control."[14] So in his Steady-State model, Daly embraces capitalism but he rejects the

---

[12] *Capitalism as if the World Mattered* (London: Earthscan, 2005), p. 84.
[13] *For the Common Good*, (Boston: Beacon, 1989), pp. 1-2; *Steady-State Economy* (Washington D.C.: Island Press, 1991), pp. 75, 100, 102, 103; *Beyond Growth* (Boston: Beacon 1996), pp. 10ff.
[14] *Steady-State Economy*, pp. 2, 54, 190-91.

consequences of market-driven economic development, especially overconsumption and environmental destruction. Now one might reasonably ask, how can he have it both ways? Daly tries to get around this contradiction by *abstracting* from the day-to-day workings of capitalism, from the demands on corporate CEOs by shareholders, from the pressures of market competition, from the implications of a no-growth capitalism for employment, and so on, and talks instead about the economy at a highly abstract meta level. So Daly says that if we are not to overdrive our ecology, there must be a "macro, social decision" about limiting the scale of growth."[15] He says that:

> "In my view, [the industrialized countries must] attain sustainability in the sense of a level of resource use that is both sufficient for a good life for its population and within the carrying capacity of the environment if generalized to the whole world. Population growth and production growth must not push us beyond the sustainable environmental capacities of resource regeneration and waste absorption. Therefore, once that point is reached, production and reproduction should be for replacement only. *Physical growth should cease, while qualitative improvement continues.*"[16]

But how could there ever be a capitalist economy that does not grow *quantitatively*? For more than 30 years Daly has chanted his mantra of "development without growth" but he has yet to explain, in any concrete way, how an actual capitalist economy comprised of capitalists, investors, employees and consumers could carry on from day to day in "stasis". Capitalist economies are, as noted above, comprised of individual producers, businesses and corporations, producing in competition with one another for sales on the market. Of course there are some, typically small, privately-owned businesses, or niche industries – farms, restaurants, mom-and-pop stores, landlords, as well as larger sole ownerships, partnerships, and family-owned businesses which can, if they so choose, carry on producing and marketing more or less the same level of output year-in year-out so long as they don't face immediate competition – because the owners of such businesses do not have to answer to other

---

[15] *Beyond Growth*, p. 16
[16] *Beyond Growth*, pp. 3, 5 (my italics).

owners – to shareholders.[17] Regulated public utilities comprise another category of enterprises that can also largely escape competitive pressures to grow because their sales, prices and profits are guaranteed and set in advance. But those are not most of the economy. Most of the economy is comprised of large corporations owned by investor-shareholders. Shareholders, even shareholders who are environmentally-minded professors investing via their TIAA-CREF accounts, are constantly seeking to maximize returns on investment. So they sensibly look to invest where they can make the highest return (these days, *any* return). This means that corporate CEOs do not have the freedom to choose to produce as much or little as they like, to make the same profits this year as last year. Instead, they face relentless pressure to maximize profits, to make more profits this year than last year (or even last quarter), therefore to maximize sales, therefore *to grow quantitatively*. So automakers, for example, look to make a profit from every car they sell. They can do this either by increasing the rate of profit on each car they sell by *intensifying* production – finding cheaper material inputs, cutting wages to lower labor costs or bringing in more efficient labor-saving technology. But they can't increase profits forever in this way. Competitors can find the same cheap inputs, the same new technology. And they can't lower wages below subsistence. So this avenue has limits. Or, they can try to maximize profits *extensively* – by selling more cars. In practice of course carmakers do both but increasing sales is normally the main avenue of profit maximization because, as Adam Smith noted, returns are theoretically limited only by the extent of the market. So facing saturated markets at home, U.S. car makers look to Asia. The same goes for any other investor-owned corporation. They're all locked into the same competitive system. In the real world, therefore, few corporations can resist the relentless pressure to "grow sales", "grow the company", "expand market share" – to *grow quantitatively*. The corporation that fails to outdo its past performance risks falling share value, stockholder flight, or worse. So Starbucks can't quench its investors thirst for profit with just coffee, even overpriced coffee, so its barristas push frappuccinos, mochaccinos, skinny cinnamon dolce lattes, CDs, movies –

---

[17] So for example, the *New York Times*, my hometown newspaper, like newspapers everywhere has been hemorrhaging money for years as advertising revenue has migrated from newsprint to the internet. But unlike so many other newspapers that have gone under in this competition, the *Times* carries on because it's a 90 percent family-owned business and the owners choose, so far at least, to continue publishing their loss-making newspaper because they're dedicated to the paper and they don't have to answer to shareholder demands to maintain profit levels. That's a luxury few businesses can afford.

whatever it takes to keep profits rising.[18] So Apple can't afford to take a breather after its huge success with its iPhone. Shareholders demand something new to propel stocks to new highs – *et voilá*: the "iPad" and the "Apple Watch" (whether you need them or not). Seen in this light, "growthmania" is hardly just a dogma, an ideology, a fetish. "Growthmania" is a rational and succinct expression of the day-to-day *requirements* of capitalist reproduction everywhere and in any conceivable capitalism.

And if economic pressures weren't sufficient to shape CEO behavior, CEOs are, in addition, legally obligated to maximize profits – *and nothing else*. So when researching his book *The Corporation*, Canadian law professor Joel Bakan interviewed Milton Friedman on the subject of the "social responsibility" and the responsibilities of executives. Friedman, channeling Adam Smith, told him that corporations are good for society but corporations should not try to *do* good for society. Bakan summed up this discussion: "Corporations are created by law and imbued with purpose by law. Law dictates what their directors and managers can do, what they cannot do, and what they must do. And, at least in the United States and other industrialized countries, the corporation, as created by law, most closely resembles Milton Friedman's ideal model of the institution: it compels executives to prioritize the interests of their companies and shareholders above all others and forbids them from being socially responsible – at least genuinely so."[19] In short, given unrelenting economic pressures and severe legal constraints, how could corporations adopt "stasis" as their maximand?

Why would anyone want a steady-state capitalism?

Of course there are times when capitalist economies do slow down, and grind along in a sort of stasis – but that's even worse. Since the fall of 2008 when the world economy suddenly ground to a halt, we've been treated to a preview of what a no-growth stasis economy would look like *under capitalism*. It's not a pretty sight: capital destruction, mass unemployment, devastated communities, foreclosures, spreading poverty and homelessness, school closures and environmental considerations shunted aside in the all-out effort to restore growth. That is "stasis"

---

[18] Keven Helliker, "At long last, customized frappuccino," *Wall Street Journal*, March 17, 2010. Julie Jargon, "Latest Starbucks concoction: juice," *Wall Street Journal*, November 11, 2011.
[19] Joel Bakan, *The Corporation* (New York: Free Press, 2004) pp. 34-35.

under capitalism. In one of his books, Daly wrote with some exasperation, "must we [grow] beyond the optimum, just to keep up the momentum of growth for the sake of avoiding unemployment?"[20] Well, yes actually, because under capitalism workers don't have job security like tenured professors. This fact may partially explain why it is that, despite all the anti-growth books published since the 1970s, *there is no public support out there for a capitalist steady-state economy.* And why should there be? Why would anyone want a steady-state *capitalist* economy? Poll after poll shows that ordinary citizens want to see the environment cleaned up, want to see a stop to the pillage of the planet, the threat of destruction of their children's future. But *as workers* in a capitalist economy, "no growth" just means no jobs. If limits to growth are imposed, and some industries have to cut back, where would laid-off workers find re-employment? And if the economy does not continuously grow (*quantitatively)*, where would the jobs come from for the workers' children? Today, in the United States, there are said to be at least seven applicants for every available job. Where are those other six people going to find jobs if there is no growth? And this situation is far worse in the developing world where unemployment levels are off the charts. So throughout the world, *given capitalism*, the only hope for workers is more growth. As a recent headline in the satirical weekly *The Onion* ran: "Masses Clamor for New Bubble."

IV. Limiting "scale"?

Daly says quite rightly that we need to reduce growth and consumption to save the humans. The way to do this, he says, is to limit the scale of "resource throughput". But what is "throughput"? Throughput, he tells us "is the flow beginning with raw materials inputs, followed by their conversion into commodities, and finally into waste outputs"[21] OK, but which resources and commodities? Do we need to limit production of meat, coal, oil, synthetic chemicals? How about Starbucks' frappuccinos, SUVs, flat-screen TVs? Ikea kitchens, jet flights to Europe, 12,000-square-foot homes? Daly doesn't tell us. He doesn't think it's necessary to specify cuts in resource use or consumption because he believes the market is the best mechanism to make these micro decisions: *"Once the level of resource throughput is reduced to a sustainable level, the pattern of consumption will automatically*

---

[20] *Steady-State Economy*, p. 101.
[21] *Beyond Growth*, p. 28. Cf. *Steady-State Economy*, p. 36.

adapt, thanks to the market. Let the market determine efficient allocation. " [22] Daly does see a role for government – to make the macro-decisions. He says that the government or "some democratically elected body" should set "controls" or "quotas" on consumption of particular resources. And the quotas, he says, "must be low enough to prevent excessive pollution and ecological costs that fall on the present as on the future."[23] But how could this ever work under capitalism?

Firstly, those quotas would have to be awfully low for some industries like, say, commercial fishing, tropical logging, even lower for the most polluting industries like coal, and virtually zero for many chemicals – if we seriously want to protect present and future human generations not to mention other species. But how could any capitalist government deliberately reduce overall consumption to a "sustainable level" and/or impose steep cuts on particular industries? Reducing consumption means reducing production. But as we noted, under capitalism, that just means recession, unemployment, falling revenues, or worse. So right now, no capitalist government on the planet is looking to do anything but *restore and accelerate* growth. That's why the U.S. Congress killed the cap and trade bill, weak as it was. That's why at Copenhagen, no capitalist government was willing to sacrifice growth to save the environment.[24] But even during the most recent, longest-sustained boom in capitalist history, no government would accept binding limits on emissions. The spectacular failures of Copenhagen, Cancun and Durban were only the latest in the long, sorry string of failures stretching all the way back to the first Rio Earth Summit in 1992. As *Nature* editorialized on the 20th anniversary of Rio, "there is little to show for 20 years of work, apart from an impressive bureaucratic machine that has been set to indefinite idle."[25]

Secondly, the ecological crisis we face is not only caused by the overall scale of production and consumption, it is *just as much* caused by the specific *irrational, inefficient, wasteful, and destructive nature of the "rational" capitalist market's "allocation of resources"* – and equally, the by market's failure to allocate resources to things we *do* need. The problem is *what we produce, what we consume,*

---

[22] *Beyond Growth*, p. 17.
[23] *Steady-State Economy*, pp. 17, 53, 65.
[24] See Jim Hansen's discussion of both Copenhagen and the U.S. climate bill in *Storms of My Grandchildren* (Bloomsbury, 12009), chapter 9.
[25] Editorial: "Back to earth," *Nature* 486, 5 (7 June 2012) on line edition at http://www.nature.com/nature/journal/v486/n7401/full/486005a.html

what we dump, what we destroy. So for example, NASA's Jim Hansen, the world's leading climate scientist, says that:

> "Coal emissions must be phased out as rapidly as possible or global climate disasters will be a dead certainty."

> "My argument is that new coal-fired power plants must be stopped as a first step toward phasing out coal emissions [and phasing out our dependence on fossil fuels]."

> "Yes, most of the fossil fuels must be left in the ground. That is the explicit message that the science provides."[26]

If we don't, we won't be able to contain global warming to within 2° Centigrade, and if we fail to do that, our goose is cooked.

After global warming, global toxic chemical pollution is almost certainly the next greatest environmental threat we face. Scientists since Rachel Carson have warned that human survival and the survival of many other species is increasingly at risk because of the growing assault on our bodies and the environment from the tens of thousands of different kinds of toxic chemicals pumped, dumped, leached, sprayed and vented into the environment every year by the chemical industry, polluting factories and farms, power plants and so forth.[27] In April 2010 the President's Cancer Panel issued a landmark 240-page report in which it said that "the true burden of environmentally induced cancers has been grossly underestimated" and strongly urged President Obama "to use the power of your office to remove the carcinogens and other toxins from our food, water, and air that needlessly increase health care costs, cripple our nation's productivity, and devastate American lives."[28] Except for lead, PCBs, DDT and a few others which have been banned or partially banned, toxic chemical pollution of all kinds has worsened dramatically in recent

---

[26] *Storms of my Grandchildren*, pp. 172, 178-9, and 236.

[27] Rachel Carson, *Silent Spring* (New York: Houghton Mifflin, 1962). Theo Colborn et al., *Our Stolen Future: Are We Threatening Our Fertility, Intelligence, and Survival?* (New York: Dutton, 1996).

[28] LaSalle D. Leffall, Jr. M.D. Chair et al. *Reducing Environmental Cancer Risk*, 2008-2009 Annual Report (U.S. Dept. of Health and Human Services, National Institutes of Health, National Cancer Institute, Washington D.C. April, 2010) at http://deainfo.nci.nih.gov/advisory/pcp/pcp08-09rpt/PCP_Report_08-09_508.pdf.

decades, all over the world, especially because of the flood of new synthetic chemicals in pesticides, plastics, fabrics, pharmaceuticals, cleaners, cosmetics, etc., and thus into our food, water and the air we breathe. The average American apple or strawberry is laced with pesticides, some of which did not exist in Rachael Carson's day.[29] America's favorite seafood, shrimp, "is a health and environmental nightmare."[30] Chemicals used in rocket fuel and dry cleaning turn up regularly in baby formula.[31] In the United States, the increasing contamination of public water supplies all over the country has become a scandal and raised alarm.[32] Everywhere we turn, we're exposed to more and more toxins.[33] Today, some 80,000 chemicals are in use in the United States, barely 200 of which have even been tested for toxicity to humans, and only a handful, actually banned. They're in our homes.[34] They're in our bodies.[35] And many are known to cause or are associated with birth defects, cancers, chronic illnesses and physical disorders, neurological disorders in children, hyperactivity and deficits in attention, developmental and reproductive problems in humans and animals – and these are on the rise around the world.

---

[29] Environmental Working Group, "A few bad apples: pesticides in your produce," April 2000 at http://www.ewg.org/reports/fewbadapples.

[30] Taras Grescoe, *Bottomfeeder: How to Eat Ethically in a World of Vanishing Seafood* (New York: Bloomsbury, 2008).

[31] Environmental Working Group (EWG) news release: "CDC: Rocket fuel chemical in most powdered infant formula," April 1, 2009 at http://www.ewg.org/node/27784.

[32] On the state of America's waters, see the *New York Times* series Toxics Waters by Charles Duhigg: "Clean water laws neglected, at a cost," September 13, 2009; "Debating just how much weed killer is safe in your water glass," August 23, 2009; "Health ills abound as farm runoff fouls wells," September 18, 2009; "Sewers at capacity, waste poisons waterways," November 23, 2009; "Millions in U.S. drink dirty water, records say," December 8, 2009; "That tap water is legal but may be unhealthy," December 17, 2009.

[33] Leslie Wayne, "Fight grows over labels on household cleaners," *New York Times, September 17, 2009.* Anjali Athavaley, "Kicking formaldehyde out of bed," *Wall Street Journal*, October 23, 2009. Joseph Pereira, "Protests spur stores to seek substitutes for vinyl in toys," *Wall Street Journal*, February 12, 2008.

[34] Leslie Kaufman and Gardiner Harris, "Environmental group reveals toxic chemicals in a range of consumer items," *New York Times,* September 17, 2009.

[35] Andrew C. Revkin, "Broad study finds lower level of old chemicals, but new trends are called worrying," *New York Times*, February 1, 2003. Anila Jacob, MD, et al. The Chemical Body Burden of Environmental Justice Leaders (Environmental Working Group, May 2009) at http://www.ewg.org/report/Pollution-in-5-Extraordinary-Women. Erika Schreder, *Earliest Exposures* (Washington Toxics Coalition, November 2009) at http://www.mnn.com/family/baby/blogs/study-finds-babies-are-exposed-to-toxic-chemicals-in-the-womb.
Bobbi Chase Wilding, Kathy Curtis, Kristen Welker-Hood, *Hazardous Chemicals in Health Care: a Snapshot of Chemicals in Doctors and Nurses* (Physicians for Social Responsibility, 2009) at http://www.psr.org/assets/pdfs/hazardous-chemicals-in-health-care.pdf.

Given that we can't anticipate all the potential risks of new synthetic chemicals, and given the scale of the problem when hundreds of new chemicals are introduced every year and many released into the environment in huge quantities, scientists like Theo Colburn and her colleagues argue that "humans as a global community" need to reconsider the convenience of synthetic chemicals like endocrine-disrupting plastics, pesticides, and other products, "against the risk they entail" and consider a drastic reduction or even a phase-out:

> "Phasing out hormone-disrupting chemicals should be just the first step, in our view. We must then move to slow down the larger experiment with synthetic chemicals. This means first curtailing the introduction of thousands of new synthetic chemicals each year. It also means reducing the use of pesticides as much as possible... *They confront us with the unavoidable question of whether to stop manufacturing and releasing synthetic chemicals altogether.* There is not glib answer, no pat recommendation to offer. The time has come, however, to pause and finally ask the ethical questions that have been overlooked in the headlong rush of the twentieth century. Is it right to change Earth's atmosphere? Is it right to alter the chemical environment in the womb of every unborn child. It is imperative that humans as a global community give serious consideration to this question and begin a broad discussion that reaches far beyond the usual participants..."[36]

So scientists are telling us that to save the humans we need to virtually shut down the coal industry, drastically reduce production of fossil fuels and phase out many toxic chemicals as quickly as possible.[37] But, how can we do this under capitalism? Peabody Coal, Chevron Oil, Monsanto – these are huge companies which have sunk all their capital and trained thousands of skilled personnel to produce what they produce. How could they just write all that off and start over? How could they accept quotas that would force them to drastically reduce production, depress profits, or even close down – and be responsible to their shareholders? As Milton Friedman said, "corporations are in business to make money, not save the world." Yet if corporations carry on with business as usual we're doomed. So what to do?

---

[36] *Our Stolen Future*, pp. 246-47 (my italics).
[37] Keith Schneider, "Science academy recommends resumption of natural farming," *New York Times*, September 8, 1989.

Beyond growth or beyond capitalism?

Lineaments of an ecological economy

If we're going to save the world, I would suggest that humanity is going to have to begin that "broad discussion" Theo Colborn proposed, with people across the whole of society and around the world to figure out how to redesign the economy. This could be the starting point of an eco-socialist economic democracy. For my part, I would suggest that an agenda for that discussion ought to include at least the following points:

(1) We're going to have to find ways to put the brakes on out-of-control growth, even if it means drastically retrenching or shutting down coal companies, oil companies, chemical companies, auto companies, even whole economic sectors dedicated 100% to waste production like the disposable products industries.

(2) We're going to have to radically restructure production by imposing sharp limits and to physically ration the use and consumption of all sorts of specific resources like coal, oil, gas, lumber, fish, oil, water, minerals, toxic chemicals and many products made from them. Some products, like coal-fired power plants, toxic pesticides, diesel fuel, bottled water and junk food should probably be phased out and banned altogether.

(3) We're going to have to sharply increase investments in things society *does* need, like renewable energy, organic farming, public transport, public water systems, public health, quality schools for our children and many other currently underfunded social and environmental needs.

(4) We're going to have to do away with production that is geared to mindless consumerism and needless repetitive consumption and the industries that support them. Too many choices and too short a lifespan for products have socially and environmentally unbearable costs. We live on a small planet with limited resources. Others need those resources too, so we can't afford waste.

(5) We're going to have to devise a rational approach to waste – meaning to minimize all waste: forbid the disposal of toxics of any sort, eliminate most (if not all) single-use products like disposable containers, wrappings, diapers, pens, cameras, etc., eliminate throwaway containers, enforce mandatory and systematic reuse of containers, packaging, recycling, composting, etc.

(6) And, if we have to shut down polluting or wasteful industries then society is going to have to provide equivalent jobs, not just retraining or the unemployment line, for those all those displaced workers because, if we don't, there will be no social support for the drastic changes we need to make to ensure our survival.

Of course, the minute we start talking about shutting down the coal industry or pesticide producers, or forcing them to change, and "directing" resources into new industries, then we're talking about violating capitalists' "freedom" to produce and sell whatever they like, and consumer "free choice" to buy whatever we want and can afford. We would be *screwing up the market*. That's right. But that is exactly what we *have to do* because the rational efficient market is very efficiently liquidating every resource on the planet and wiping us out in the process. If we want to save ourselves and many other species, then we have to give up the freedom of capitalists to produce and sell as they please and consumers to buy whatever they like and can afford – *in order to win the greater freedom* for humanity to breathe clean air, to have safe water to drink, to have safe food to eat, to live long and healthy lives free of toxics-induced diseases, to restore a forested, clean, safe, habitable planet we can pass on to our children. Such a democratic and ecological economy would of course be completely incompatible with capitalist property and capitalist organization of production. It would in fact require large-scale democratic planning of the entire economy.

V. Daly's misplaced faith in the market

Daly rejects any such interference with market organization of production because, like his mainstream colleagues, he believes that "the market is the most efficient institution we have come up with" and the only option we have.[38] He can say this because he subscribes to a capitalist conception of efficiency. Capitalist economists since Adam Smith have defined economic efficiency from the standpoint of the *production unit* – the factory, mill, mine, etc. (which, conveniently, the capitalists own). So in capitalist terms, the most efficient production method, technology, or economic system is the one that gets the most output from the least input, so produces the cheapest widgets and generates the most product/sales/wealth for a given investment of labor and raw materials. So Daly says the market "is wonderful

---

[38] *Steady-State Economy*, p. 51. *For the Common Good*, pp. 14, 19, 44-47; and *Beyond Growth*, pp. 13-14, 17.

for allocation". "Markets singlemindedly aim to serve allocative efficiency."[39] Since markets are such efficient allocators of resources, Daly believes that the role of the state should just be to:

> "impose... quantitative limits on aggregate throughput... within which the market can safely function, *and then the market is left alone*."[40]

But what exactly does this mean? Efficient for what end? Optimal for whom? And by leaving the corporations "alone" to maximize capitalist efficiency and optimality according to their interests, doesn't this just open the way to further social and environmental destruction, and thus to undermine Daly's social and environmental goals?

So if, for example, mountaintop removal is the most efficient method of getting the most coal out of the ground at the cheapest price (which it seems to be), but this system is based on horrific environmental destruction – not unlike war – with exploding mountains flooding, burying and devastating whole communities, towns and counties, poisoning water supplies, wrecking local economies throughout Appalachia, and adding new health problems to already burdened communities – while the very efficiency of production itself only serves to lower the cost of coal, promote increased coal combustion, and thus accelerate global warming – what is so optimal and wonderful about this free market allocation of resources? Who cares if mountaintop removal is the most cost-efficient allocation of resources if what they're producing is killing us?[41]

If satellite-guided fishing trawlers, with nets the size of several football fields, are the most efficient means of maximizing the fish catch at the lowest possible price, but this strip-mining of the oceans has wiped out fishery after fishery, depleting many global fisheries to the point of extinction, even starving dolphins and seals, while wrecking the ocean bottoms, demolishing coral reefs and destroying deep

---

[39] *Beyond Growth*, pp. 13, 32 (italics in original). Daly quoted in Porrit, *op. cit.*, p. 78, (my italics); *For The Common Good*, pp. 44-49.
[40] *Steady-State Economics*, pp. 88-89 (my italics).
[41] See e.g. Tom Butler et al. eds., *Plundering Appalachia: The Tragedy of Mountaintop Removal Coal Mining* (San Rafael, CA: Palace Press Intl.: 2009) and, again, James Hansen *op. cit.*

water ecologies – what is optimal about this market allocation of resources from the standpoint of humanity, nature and future generations of fish – and fish eaters?[42]

If toxic chemical companies like Monsanto or Dupont manufacture Roundup or Benlate at the highest level of technical efficiency, in the cleanest factories, with the least waste going out the back door, what does this matter if the products they send out the front door and spray all over the planet are helping to extinguish life on earth? What kind of lunatic efficiency and optimality is this?[43]

If most of the American economy – from cars to appliances, from furniture to decoration, from fashion and cosmetics to throw-away this and that – and all their supporting industries and services like advertising, credit cards, packaging, etc., etc. – are geared to *insatiable repetitive consumption*, to driving consumers to, as retailing analyst Victor Lebow described it back in the 1950s, "use up, wear out, burn up, and discard" perfectly good cars, TVs, clothes, phones and buy something "new" and "up-to-date" even if what they have already is perfectly useful, even if the new replacement is trivially different, in an endless and ever-growing cycle of planned obsolescence and "forced consumption" what is optimal and efficient, let alone wonderful, about all this – given the state of the world's depleted resources today?[44]

Now Herman Daly would never want to see the sorts of awful, irrational, wasteful and destructive free-market resource allocations I've just described turn up in his Steady-State Economy. But aren't such corporate practices guaranteed to be there? Since in Daly's model of a steady-state capitalism, the government's role is only to set an upper limit on throughput consumption and then get out of the way, leaving the market "alone" and in charge, why would the market act any differently than it does right now?

---

[42] See e.g. Michael Berrill, *The Plundered Seas* (San Francisco: Sierra Club, 1997).
[43] See Marie-Monique Robin, director, *The World According to Monsanto* (National Film Board of Canada et al., 2008) and her book of the same title by The New Press, 2009.
[44] The quoted phrases Victor Lebow were cited by Vance Packard in *The Waste Makers* (New York: David McKay, 1960) pp. 24, 33.

Beyond growth or beyond capitalism?

Eco-socialist efficiency vs. capitalist efficiency

There is a place for efficiency in an ecological economy. After all, no one wants to waste labor or natural resources. But when, as under capitalism, the whole point of using resources efficiently is just to use the saved resources to produce even more commodities, to accelerate the conversion of *even more* natural resources into products – to be "used up, worn out, burned up, and discarded" so the cycle can begin all over again – capitalist efficiency turns into its opposite. In the 1860s, the English economist William Jevons famously observed that gains in technological efficiency – specifically, the more economical use of coal in engines doing mechanical work – actually increased the overall consumption of coal, iron and other resources, rather than "saving" them, as many had hoped (because British officials were already growing concerned about running out of coal). As he wrote:

> "It is the very economy of its use which leads to its extensive consumption... [E]very... improvement of the engine, when effected, does but accelerate anew the consumption of coal."[45]

This "rebound" or "backfire" was not a function of technological improvement *per se*. Under different social arrangements, if profit were not the goal of production, then such gains in efficiency could indeed save these natural resources for the benefit of society and future generations. But Jevons lived and we live under capitalism. In this system cheaper inputs only give producers greater incentive to "grow the market" by selling more product at lower prices to more consumers and thus to push sales and profits still higher. So, ironically, the very capitalist efficiency and market organization of production that Daly celebrates just brings on the growth and further environmental destruction he so dreads.

But if we consider efficiency from the standpoint of *society and ecology*, including future as well as present generations – instead of just from the standpoint of the production unit – then the definition of efficiency is completely the opposite of market efficiency. So from a social-ecological perspective, it would be absurdly

---

[45] William Stanley Jevons, *The Coal Question, 3rd edn.* (New York: Kelley, 1905) p. 140-41, 152-53, cited in Blake Alcott, "Jevon's paradox, *Journal of Ecological Economics*, 54 (2005) p. 12. Even pro-industry Frances Cairncross notes that in the chemical industry "[t]hroughout the 1980s, companies like Dow and BASF steadily cut effluent per ton of product sold, but their final sales increased." So pollution increased even as they "cleaned up". *Costing the Earth* (London: The Economist Books Ltd., 1992) p. 269.

inefficient to waste resources producing goods and services we don't need, to produce goods designed to wear out or become obsolete as fast as possible – just so we can do the same work all over again. Why would we want to do that? It would be so much more efficient and less wasteful to build cars, appliances, computers etc. to be as *durable* and *long lasting* as possible, to need as *few* "model" changes as necessary, to be as *upgradable* and *rebuildable* as possible – and take longer vacations. From society's standpoint, it would be not just inefficient, but suicidal to keep running coal-fired power plants that are killing us, just because capital is sunk into them. It would be far less costly to society and the environment, for society to collectively absorb the cost of phasing these out and replacing these plants with renewable technologies we already have. From society's standpoint, it would be ruinous to contaminate the country's topsoil, pollute our public water supplies and poison ourselves with an endless array of toxic pesticides and other synthetic chemicals, just to produce corn or soybeans a few cents cheaper per bushel for a decade or so until the soil is completely exhausted and poisoned. If Monsanto can't afford to shut down its production of toxics, society could afford to close down those polluting plants and find other, better, employment for those talented and skilled but mis-allocated chemists and workers. And even if society decides that it needs some synthetic chemicals, to some extent, an eco-social chemical policy would start from the Precautionary Principle such as has already been elaborated by scientists, doctors and grass-roots anti-toxics organizations like Safer Chemicals Healthy Families, which calls for: safer substitutes and solutions; a phase-out of persistent bioaccumulative or highly toxic chemicals; publication of full right-to-know and rights of workers and communities to participate in decisions on chemicals; publication of comprehensive safety data on all chemicals; and insistence on the immediate priority protection of communities and workers in the event of any threat.[46]

VI. Beyond capitalism

Daly and the anti-growth school are certainly right that we need to break out of the "iron cage of consumerism", "downshift" to a simpler life, find meaning and self-realization in promoting the common good instead of accumulating stuff. They call

---

[46] See the Louisville Charter and its background papers at http://www.louisvillecharger.org/thecharter.shml; and the publications of Safer Chemicals Healthy Families at http://www.saferchemicals.org.

for an environmentally rational economy that conserves nature and resources for the benefit of our children and theirs, instead of consuming the whole planet right now. They call for a redistribution of wealth to those in need, and for the construction of a society based, not on possessive individualism, but on a decent material sufficiency for everyone on the planet. And they call for a moral and spiritual transformation of our values away from materialism. Those are laudable goals. But we can't do any of those things under capitalism because under capitalism, we're all just rats racing in Paul Krugman's cages. We can't stop consuming more and more because if we stop racing, the system collapses into crisis. So it follows, I submit, that we need a completely different kind of economic system, a non-capitalist economic system based on human needs, environmental needs, and a completely different value system – not on profit. Ecological economists from Herman Daly to Tim Jackson have called for a "new macro-economic model" a "new vision", a "new paradigm", a "new central organizing principle". But all they actually offer us are unworkable, warm and fuzzy capitalist utopias, with no plausible means of escaping the iron cage of consumerism or the "growthmania" of the market. Jonathon Porrit says that "like it or not" we have to try to find sustainability within a "capitalist framework" and forget about alternatives. But if the engine of capitalist growth and consumption can't be stopped, or even throttled back, and if the logic of capitalist efficiency and capitalist rationality is killing us, what choice to we have but to rethink the theory? Like it or not Jonathon, it's time to abandon the fantasy of a steady-state capitalism, go back to the drawing boards and come up with a *real* "new macro-economic model", a practical, workable post-capitalist ecological economy – an economy by the people, for the people, that is geared to production for need, not for profit. "Socialism"? "Economic democracy"? Call it what you like. But what other choice do we have? Either we save capitalism or we save ourselves. We can't save both.

Green capitalism: the god that failed

ESSAY 3 (2011)

Green capitalism: the god that failed

Abstract In rejecting the antigrowth approach of the first wave of environmentalists in the 1970s, pro-growth "green capitalism" theorists of the 1980s-90s like Paul Hawken, Lester Brown, and Francis Cairncross argued that green technology, green taxes, eco-conscious shopping and the like could "align" profit-seeking with environmental goals, even "invert many fundamentals" of business practice such that "restoring the environment and making money become one and the same process." This strategy has clearly failed. I claim first, that the project of sustainable capitalism was misconceived and doomed from the start because maximizing profit and saving the planet are inherently in conflict and cannot be systematically aligned even if, here and there, they might coincide for a moment. That's because under capitalism, CEOs and corporate boards are not responsible to society, they're responsible to private shareholders. CEOs can embrace environmentalism so long as this increases profits. But saving the world requires that the pursuit of profits be systematically subordinated to ecological concerns: For example, the science says that to save the humans, we have to drastically cut fossil fuel consumption, even close down industries like coal. But no corporate board can sacrifice earnings to save the humans because to do so would be to risk shareholder flight or worse. I claim that profit-maximization is an iron rule of capitalism, a rule that trumps all else, and this sets the limits to ecological reform -- and not the other way around as green capitalism theorists supposed.

Secondly, I claim that contrary to green capitalism proponents, across the spectrum from resource extraction to manufacturing, the practical possibilities for "greening" and "dematerializing" production are severely limited. This means, I contend, that the only way to prevent overshoot and collapse is to enforce a massive economic contraction in the industrialized economies, retrenching production across a broad range of unnecessary, resource-hogging, wasteful and polluting industries, even virtually shutting down the worst. Yet this option is foreclosed under capitalism because this is not socialism: no one is promising new jobs to unemployed coal miners, oil-drillers, automakers, airline pilots, chemists, plastic junk makers, and others whose jobs would be lost because their industries would have to be retrenched -- and unemployed workers don't pay taxes. So CEOs, workers, and governments find that they all "need" to maximize growth, overconsumption, even pollution, to destroy their childrens' tomorrows to hang onto their jobs today because, if they don't, the system falls into crisis, or worse. So we're all onboard the TGV of ravenous and ever-growing plunder and pollution. And as our locomotive races toward the cliff of ecological collapse, the only thoughts on the minds of our CEOS, capitalist economists, politicians and labor leaders is how to stoke the locomotive to get us there faster. Corporations aren't necessarily evil. They just can't help themselves. They're doing what they're supposed to do for the benefit of their owners. But this means that, so long as the global economy is based on capitalist private/corporate property and competitive production for market, we're doomed to collective social suicide and no amount of tinkering with the market can brake the drive to global ecological collapse. We can't shop our way to sustainability because the problems we face cannot be solved by individual choices in the marketplace. They require collective democratic control over the economy to prioritize the needs of society and the environment. And they require national and international economic planning to re-organize the economy and redeploy labor and resources to these ends. I conclude, therefore, that if humanity is to save itself, we have no choice but to overthrow capitalism and replace it with a democratically-planned socialist economy.

I. Saving the Earth for fun and profit

In rejecting the antigrowth "limits" approach of the first wave of environmentalism in the 1970s, pro-market, pro-growth "green capitalism" theorists of the 1980s and

Green capitalism: the god that failed

90s such as Paul Hawken, Lester Brown and Francis Cairncross argued that green technology, green taxes, green labeling, eco-conscious shopping and the like could "align" profit-seeking with environmental goals, even "invert many fundamentals" of business practice such that "restoring the environment and making money become one and the same process."[1] This turn to the market was an expression of broader trends from the 1980s in which activists retreated from collective action to change society, in favor of individualist approaches to trying to save the world by embracing market forces – "shopping our way to sustainability."[2] In the market mania of the Reagan-Clinton era, Herman Daly's plea for imposing "limits to growth" came to seem dated – like Birkenstocks and Bucky Fuller's geodesic dome houses. Many American environmentalists bought into the "doing well by doing good" message of green capitalism because there had never been much of a left or socialist presence in the American environmental movement beyond a small anarchist fringe, unlike Europe where many, if not most, greens were also reds. So it was easy for American environmentalists to go with the market – and there were jobs. Protesting didn't pay the rent. Some became eco-entrepreneurs. Some got jobs in one or other of the new green capitalist ventures from organic foods and markets, to renewable energy startups, eco-travel outfits, "socially responsible investment" banking, "green labeling" outfits that "certified" lumber, fair-trade coffee, and so on. Most connected with mainstream environmental NGOs like the Sierra Club that focused on lobbying the government. In these and other ways, through the 80s and 90s, protesting gradually gave way to lobbying and green capitalism.

"There is no polite way to say that business is destroying the world".[3]

---

[1] Paul Hawken, *Ecological Commerce* (New York: HarperCollins, 1993); Paul Hawken, Amory Lovins, L. Hunter Lovins, *Natural Capitalism* (Boston: Little Brown and Co.: 1999); Lester R. Brown, *Eco-Economy* (New York: Norton, 2001), Jonathan Porrit, *Capitalism as if the World Mattered* (London: Earthscan, 2005); Frances Cairncross, *Costing the Earth* (Boston: Harvard Business School Press, 1992) and *Green, Inc.* (Washington D.C.: Island Press, 1995); James Gustave Speth, *The Bridge at the End of the World* (New Haven: Yale University Press, 2008). Nicholas Stern, *The Economics of Climate Change* (Cambridge: CUP, 2007) restates many of these ideas.
[2] On this history see Andrew Szaz, *Shopping Our Way to Safety: How We Changed From Protecting the Environment to Protecting Ourselves* (Minneapolis: University of Minnesota Press, 2007).
[3] *The Ecology of Commerce,* 1993, p.3 – my italics.

Green capitalism: the god that failed

Of all the eco-futurist writers of the 1980s and 90s, entrepreneur and "Natural Capitalism" guru Paul Hawken has probably been the most influential voice for eco-capitalism. Hailed by *Inc.* magazine as *"the poet laureate of American capitalism"*, Hawken says he was inspired to pen his best seller *Ecology of Commerce* (1993) when his company Smith & Hawken won the prestigious Environmental Stewardship Award from the Council on Economic Priorities in 1991. When George Plimpton presented the award to Smith & Hawken at New York's Waldorf-Astoria Hotel, Hawken says he:

> "...looked out over the sea of pearls and black ties, suddenly realizing two things: first that my company did not deserve the award and second, that no one else did either. What we had done was scratch the surface of the problem... but in the end the impact on the environment was only marginally different than if we had done nothing at all. The recycled toner cartridges, the sustainably harvested woods, the replanted trees, the soy-based inks, and the monetary gifts to nonprofits were all well and good, but basically we were in the junk mail business, selling products by catalogue. All the recycling in the world would not change the fact that [this] is an energy intensive endeavor that gulps down resources."

For the reality, Hawken said, was that:

> "Despite all this good work, we still must face a sobering fact. If every company on the planet were to adopt the best environmental practices of the "leading" companies – say, the Body Shop, Patagonia, or 3M – the world would still be moving toward sure degradation and collapse... Quite simply, our business practices are destroying life on earth. Given current corporate practices, not one wildlife preserve, wilderness, or indigenous culture will survive the global market economy. We know that every natural system on the planet is disintegrating. The land, water, air, and sea have been functionally transformed from life-supporting systems into repositories for waste. *There is no polite way to say that business is destroying the world."*[4]

---

[4] *The Ecology of Commerce* (New York: Harper, 1993), preface and p. 3 (my italics).

So business is destroying the world. But, for Hawken, the problem wasn't capitalism as such but just bad "business practices" of corporations which, he thought, could be fundamentally "inverted" to save the world: "[T]his behavior is not the inherent nature of business, nor the inevitable outcome of a free-market system." The problem was that "the expense of destroying the earth is largely absent from the prices set in the marketplace. A vital and key piece of information is therefore missing in all levels of the economy."[5] The key was to get the market to "tell the ecological truth". In her Harvard Business School manifesto for green capitalism, *Costing the Earth*, the *Economist* magazine's environmental editor Francis Cairncross said, "Governments need to step in to align private costs with social costs... [as] embodied the 'polluter pays' principle."[6] And in his book *Eco-Economy*, Worldwatch Institute founder Lester Brown explained that, "Ecologists and economists – working together – can calculate the ecological costs of various economic activities. These costs could then be incorporated into the market price of a product or service in the form of a tax." So carbon taxes and the like would "discourage such activities as coal burning", "the generation of toxic waste, the use of virgin raw materials", "the use of pesticides, and the use of throwaway products".[7] Paul Hawken even went so far as to claim that:

> *"[T]here is no question that we could introduce a steady, incremental phase-in of a carbon tax on coal, one that would eventually tax coal out of business in two decade's time...* The whole key to redesigning the economy is to shift incrementally most if not all of the taxes presently derived from 'goods' to 'bads,' from income and payroll taxes to taxes on pollution, environmental degradation, and nonrenewable energy consumption... The resulting changes in the marketplace would be dramatic. Every purchase would become more constructive and less destructive."

Hawken described his vision of "Natural Capitalism" thusly:

---

[5] *Ibid.*, pp. 15, 13
[6] *Costing the Earth*, p. 89.
[7] *Ecological Economics*, pp. 234-36, my italics

"The restorative economy described in this book... unites ecology and commerce into one sustainable act of production and distribution that mimics and enhances natural processes.

"In such an economy... restoring the environment and making money would be the same process. Business... needs a plan, a vision, a basis – a broad social mandate that will turn it away from the linear, addictive, short-term economic activities in which it is enmeshed and trapped... Rather than argue about where to put our wastes, who will pay for it, and how long it will be before toxins leak out into the groundwater, we should be trying to design systems that are elegantly imitative of climax ecosystems found in nature. Companies must re-envision and re-imagine themselves as cyclical corporations, whose products either literally disappear into harmless components, or... [produce] no waste [at all.]"[8]

NRDC founder and Yale Dean, Gus Speth summed up this utopian vision of the market in "green capitalism" as well as anyone:

"The market can be transformed into an instrument for environmental restoration; humanity's ecological footprint can be reduced to what can be sustained environmentally; the incentives that govern corporate behavior can be rewritten; growth can be focused on things that truly need to grow and consumption on having enough, not always on more; the rights of future generations and other species can be respected."[9]

The "sustainable" "green" "natural" capitalism movement took off in the 1980s and 90s. Organic farming came into the mainstream and Whole Foods became the fastest growing sector of the grocery industry. Green businesses sprouted up in every sector from renewable energy to organic cottons to eco-travel. Stores added green products in every aisle. Hip, eco-conscious businesses like Patagonia gave "1% to nature". (Ben & Jerry's gave 7.5%!) "Sustainable investing" mutual funds looked to fund renewable energy. "Green certification" outfits sprung up to save the tropical forests and the sea turtles. Eventually, even big corporations like 3M and Wallmart

---

[8] *Ecology of Commerce*, pp. 3, 11-12, 54-55.
[9] *Bridge at the End of the World*, p. 12. See also pp. 180-191.

embraced green "business practices" cutting waste, recycling, producing and adopting less toxic products. Europe introduced the first large-scale cap and trade system in January 2005. Finland introduced the first carbon tax in 1990 and many other countries followed suite including Sweden, Germany, Britain, South Korea, South Africa, Korea, some provinces of Canada, and even some American states including Maryland, Colorado, and California.

The green capitalist god that failed

There can be no doubt that we are better off for many of these initiatives. But two decades on, for all the organic groceries, energy efficient lightbulbs, appliances and buildings, carbon trading and carbon taxes, the global ecology is collapsing faster than ever. Climate change, as Bill McKibben tells us in his new book, *eaarth*, is no longer a distant threat; it's already upon us. CO_2 and other greenhouse gas emissions are currently growing at *four times* the rate they grew in the 1990s. 2010 was the hottest year on record and the 2000s the hottest decade on record. From peat fires around Moscow to huge floods in Pakistan, super hurricanes, super storms, super winter snowfalls and floods or, alternately, extended drought (even both in Australia), are becoming the norm. Seas are rising and ice is melting faster than scientists imagined possible even as recently as 2007. Tropical forests continue to fall. Glacier melt is accelerating around the world with dire implications for agriculture from India to China, California to Peru. Rivers are drying up. Soil depletion continues unabated. Water tables are falling relentlessly around the world. Drought has become a permanent feature of the American southwest, of Australia, of regions of Africa and the Middle East, and northern China. Ocean fisheries are collapsing right and left. Coral reefs, scientists now think, could die off in many places by mid-century and over the entire planet by 2100. Penguin colonies are at risk. The collective impact of nearly 7 billion people pumping their emissions into the atmosphere and dumping their excreta and toxics into drains and rivers that eventually issue into the seas, is actually changing the chemical composition of the world's vast oceans, threatening the future both of living creatures in the oceans and those who live off the oceans. We're destroying life and wiping out species so fast that, in Bill McKibben's words, "We're running Genesis backward, decreating."[10] In short, for all the green initiatives, corporate business practices have changed little – or the little they've changed has had no great effect. From Kyoto to Cancun,

---

[10] See Bill McKibben's review of our current status in *eaarth* (New York: Henry Holt, 2010), chapter one, from which much of this paragraph is drawn.

governments have all made it abundantly clear that they will not accept binding limits on greenhouse gas emissions; they will not sacrifice growth today to save the planet tomorrow. Europe's cap and trade scheme, the first large scale effort, enriched traders and polluters but failed to put the brakes on the relentless rise of greenhouse gas emissions. What few carbon taxes governments actually imposed have likewise failed to stem emissions. At the end of the day, the project of green capitalism has failed and its proponents are in disarray.

II. Delusions of "natural capitalism"

Paul Hawken was right. We need a "restorative economy", an economy that lives within nature's limits, that minimizes and even eliminates waste from production, and so on. But he was completely wrong to imagine that we could ever get this under capitalism. In what follows I am going to explain why this is so and in conclusion state what I think are the implications of this critique. To start with, I'm going to state five theses about green capitalism and then develop these arguments in the rest of this essay.

1. Capitalism and saving the planet are fundamentally and irreconcilably at odds. It is not just "bad business practices". Profit seeking cannot be *systematically* "aligned" with environmental goals, much less subordinated, because any corporate CEO who attempts to do so (and we shall consider the fate of some who tried) will shortly find himself in hot water with his bosses, the shareholders, or if he were to persist, his company would be driven out of the market and/or abandoned by its shareholders. I argue therefore, that the only way to systematically align production with society's needs is to do so directly, in a democratically planned economy.

2. No capitalist government on Earth can impose "green taxes" that would drive the coal industry – or any other industry – out of business, or even force major retrenchments by suppressing production because, among other important reasons, given capitalism, this would just provoke recession and mass unemployment, if not worse. This means the carbon tax strategy to stop global warming is a non-starter. Since profit seeking and environmental goals are systematically opposed, without green taxes, the entire green capitalist project collapses.

3. Green capitalism enthusiasts vastly underestimate the gravity, scope and speed of the global ecological collapse we face and thus unrealistically imagine that growth can continue forever if we just tweak the incentives and penalties a bit here and there with green taxes and such. I claim that the capitalist market system is inherently eco-suicidal, that endless growth can only end in catastrophic eco-collapse, that no amount of tinkering can alter the market system's suicidal trajectory, and that, therefore, like it or not, humanity has no choice but to try to find a way to replace capitalism with some kind of post-capitalist ecologically sustainable economy.

4. Green capitalism theorists grossly overestimate the potential of "clean" "green" production and "dematerializing", the economy whereas, in reality, much if not most of the economy – from resource extraction like mining and drilling, to metals smelting and chemicals production, to most manufacturing – cannot be greened in any meaningful sense at all. This means that if we really want to dramatically reduce greenhouse gas emissions by the 80% that scientists say we need to do to save the humans, then we have no choice but to enforce a *drastic contraction of production* in the industrialized countries, especially in the most polluting and wasteful sectors. Most industries will have to be sharply retrenched. Some, the very worst polluting and wasteful, will have to be virtually closed down entirely. Since the scale of the cuts we need to make to save the humans would mean mass unemployment under capitalism, I contend that the only way to address this problem is to construct a bottom-up socialist economic democracy that can guarantee employment to those made redundant by retraction and closures. Further, the need for sharp cutbacks in production will mean less work overall, therefore the necessity of sharing what work there is among all workers, therefore a shortening of the working day, a sharing economy, all of which will be necessary to save the humans but none of which are compatible with capitalism.

5. Consumerism and overconsumption are not "dispensable" and cannot be exorcised because they're not just "cultural" or "habitual". They are built into capitalism and indispensable for the day-to-day reproduction of corporate producers in a competitive market system in which capitalists, workers, consumers and governments alike are all dependent upon an endless cycle of perpetually increasing consumption to maintain profits,

jobs, and tax revenues. We can't shop our way to sustainability because the problems we face cannot be solved by individual choices in the marketplace because, among other reasons, the global ecological crisis we face cannot be solved by even the largest individual companies, especially because many of these companies will have to be shut down altogether, and furthermore, many problems such as global warming, overfishing, ocean chemistry, are beyond the scope of nation states. They require collective bottom-up, democratic control over the entire world economy; they require national and international economic planning, national and global redistributions of wealth to maximize popular support for necessary changes, and global economic coordination to prioritize the needs of humanity, other life forms, and the environment.

IIA. The folly of "cap and trade" and carbon taxes

Green capitalism's problems start with the failure of "cap and trade" schemes and the refusal of countries to adopt green taxes of real significance. By the end of the first decade of the 21st century, it was evident that the world's first efforts at CO_2 and other greenhouse gas mitigation, the voluntary approach embodied in the 1997 Kyoto Protocols, was a failure. The Kyoto Protocol obliged the industrialized countries to cut carbon emissions by an average of 5.2 percent below 1990 levels by 2008-2012. Virtually no country honestly lived up to its promises. For example, Japan, the strongest promoter of the Kyoto Protocol, promised to reduce emissions 6 percent below 1990 levels by 2008. Instead, by 2009 Japan's emissions *exceeded* its 1990 levels by 9 percent. Most of the rest of the world did much worse than that. Emissions skyrocketed.[11] By 2006, scientists reported that global emissions were then rising four times faster than they were a decade earlier. An alarming 13 of the 15 original EU signers of the accords increased their emissions, many sharply. Germany did better, almost meeting its target, but only because it incorporated East Germany and thus bettered its average by closing down dirty, inefficient communist-era plants. The U.K. also did better but only because North Sea gas discoveries enabled it to close coal mines and replace coal-fired power with gas – a situation

---

[11] See Jim Hansen's summary of Kyoto's failures in his *Storms of My Grandchildren* (New York: Bloomsbury, 2010), pp. 182-83, and p. 206.

that is unlikely to last because North Sea gas peaked in 1999 and will be two-thirds gone by 2015.[12]

No green capitalism in one country

Kyoto failed because, given a competitive globalized world market, for some countries to sign on these obligations while others – conspicuously the U.S., China, and India – did not, was to commit economic suicide. Analysts predicted that if they abided by Kyoto's requirements, the UK's GDP would fall by 1 percent by 2010, Italy's by 2 percent, Spain's by 3 percent and all three countries would lose at least 200,000 jobs each.[13] This is why, already by 2005, even ardent advocates of Kyoto were bailing out. So Tony Blair, erstwhile hardcore Kyoto fan, told the Clinton Global Initiative in September 2005 that *"I'm changing my thinking on this. . . No country is going to cut its growth or consumption substantially in the light of a long-term environmental problem."*[14]

II.A.1. "Cap and trade": the market solution to Kyoto's failed voluntary limits solution

In the wake of Kyoto's failures, many economists and environmentalists embraced "cap and trade" schemes which, they claimed, would overcome the weaknesses of Kyoto's voluntary approach by relying instead on market incentives and penalties. The cap and trade idea was that governments would set ceilings on maximum allowable CO_2 emissions – the cap – for a given set of polluting industries. Then, for every ton of CO_2 that a polluter reduces under the cap, it is awarded one "permit" to pollute. Permits could be bought, sold, traded or banked for the future. Any plant that cut its emissions below the mandated level could sell their excess allowances to overpolluters. Overpolluters could buy these indulgences and keep on polluting. But over time, governments would ratchet down the cap, restricting allowances. This would drive up the cost of permits. Dirty plants would face rising costs to keep buying permits to keep operating. Efficient plants would profit from clean

---

[12] Cited in Mark Lynas, *Six Degrees* (New York: National Georgraphic/Harpers, 2008), pp. 269-70.

[13] Dana Joel Gattuso, "Kyoto's anniversary: little reason to celebrate," February 2006 (Washington D.C.: The National Center for Public Policy Research) at http://www.nationalcenter.org/NPA537EuropeKyoto206.html.

[14] Tony Blair, Remarks, Clinton Global Initiative, Special Opening Plenary Session (New York), September 15, 2005, quoted in *ibid.*

technology. Eventually, as permit prices rose, fossil fuel costs would exceed renewable energy prices and fossil fuels use would pass from the scene. The theory had a certain elegance. But all the same, greenhouse gas cap and trade schemes failed just like Kyoto. The problem this time was that the "cap" was really a cap – a finite limit on emissions.[15] But in a globalized market, governments are loathe to undermine the competitiveness of their own industries or restrain growth by imposing finite limits on emissions. So in Europe, where the first mandatory trading market was established in 2005, governments (according to one report) were "beseeched by giant utilities and smokestack industries that feared for their competitiveness..."[16] In Germany, industry lobbyists badgered the government for higher caps, special exceptions of all sorts, they warned of unemployment, threatened to pack up and leave Germany, and so on. In the end, governments caved. Jürgen Tritten, former Green Party leader and German minister of environment from 1998 to 2005, recalled being lobbied by executives from power companies, and by politicians from the former East Germany seeking special treatment for lignite, a highly polluting soft brown coal common in central Europe. Handing out permits, he says he felt "like a grandfather with a large family deciding what to give his favorite children for Christmas". Mr Trittin recalled a five-hour "showdown" with Wolfgang Clement, then economy minister, in which he lost a battle to lower the overall limit. Clement reproached the Greens saying that "at the end of their policy there is the de-industrialization of Germany".[17] Similarly, in confrontation with the Federation of German Electricity Companies, "good sense triumphed in the end" and industry won. Whereas under EU commitments, German electricity companies were supposed to receive 3 percent fewer permits than they needed to cover their total emissions between 2005 and 2007, which would have obliged them to cut emissions by that amount, instead the companies got 3 percent *more* than they needed – a windfall worth about $374 billion dollars at that time. As governments caved, emissions soared, and the profits went to the polluters and the traders. As the *New York Times* described the process:

> "The European Union started with a high-minded ecological goal: encouraging companies to cut their greenhouse gases by making them pay for each ton of carbon dioxide they emitted into the

---

[15] Hansen, *Storms*, p.213.
[16] James Kanter and Jad Mouawad, "Money and lobbyists hurt European efforts to curb gases," *New York Times*, December 11, 2010
[17] *Ibid.*

atmosphere. But that plan unleashed a lobbying free-for-all that led politicians to dole out favors to various industries, undermining the environmental goals. Four years later, it is becoming clear that system has so far produced little noticeable benefit to the climate — *but generated a multibillion-dollar windfall for some of the Continent's biggest polluters.*"[18]

Everyone needs higher caps, special exemptions, temporary relief. And so it goes. With Europe's cap and trade plans in tatters, Obama dropped his own cap and trade plan, once the centerpiece of his environmental campaign platform. In 2010 Japan and South Korea shelved their proposed plans to start cap and trade schemes in 2013 under heavy pressure from businesses that complained it was unfair to burden them with such costs when the U.S. and China refused to do the same.[19] Australia has officially put off any decision on carbon-trading until 2013. And so it goes.

II.A.2. Carbon taxes: the market solution to the failed cap-and-trade market solution

Critics of cap and trade, like Al Gore and NASA's Jim Hansen,[20] have argued for a simpler, more transparent, direct approach that supposedly cuts out all the profiteering – a flat carbon tax. No more lobbying. No more loopholes. In Jim Hansen's words: "All sweet deals will be wiped off the books by a uniform carbon fee at the sources, which will affect all fossil fuel uses."[21] But carbon taxes are no more a solution to curbing greenhouse gases than cap and trade. Contradictions abound. For a start, green taxes have proven no more immune to "sweet deals" than were the cap and trade schemes. Dozens of countries and local governments have introduced carbon taxes since 1990, but these have not led to significant declines in emissions in most of these countries. That's because, everywhere, industries lobbied to keep taxes low (instead of caps high), various groups demanded exemptions, unions resisted taxes that could cost jobs, consumers resisted new taxes. So when finally introduced, after all the negotiations, carbon taxes have been too low to effect much change: pollution is taxed but not enough to stop it, or even reduce it by much.

[18] *Ibid.*, my italics.
[19] "East Asian cap and trade plans hit the wall," January 18, 2011, *Carbonpositive* at http://www.carbonpositive.net/viewarticle.aspx?articleID=2235
[20] See Jim Hansen's arguments for a carbon tax in *Storms*, p. 215ff. For Al Gore's arguments see his *Our Choice* (Emanus, PA: Rodale, 2009), pp. 342-45.
[21] *Storms*, p. 210.

Green capitalism: the god that failed

The French case illustrates all of these problems: Nicolas Sarkozy sought to push France into the lead of the fight "to save the human race" (after all, this is France) by implementing a carbon tax in 2009. But days before the tax was to take effect, a French court ruled it unconstitutional because it would have let off most industrial polluters entirely plus it allowed generous discounts and exceptions to various sectors such as truckers, farmers, fishing fleets, while placing a disproportionately heavy burden on ordinary households. The court said that more than 1,000 of France's biggest polluters could have been exempted from the charges, and that 93 percent of industrial emissions would not have been taxed.[22] But even if Sarkozy had successfully imposed his carbon tax, this tax would have raised the price of gasoline by just 25 US cents per gallon. Given that the French already pay nearly $9 per gallon for gasoline, it's hard to see how an additional 25 cents would seriously discourage consumption let alone "save the human race". Jim Hansen proposes a carbon tax of $1 per gallon of gasoline in the U.S. But given that gasoline prices in the U.S. are much less than half the cost of those in Europe, so cheap that that gas-guzzling 7,000-pound "Suburbans" 6000-pound "light trucks" and bloated over-accessorized luxury cars are the best selling vehicles in the U.S., it's hard to imagine how tacking another buck onto a gallon of gas is going to change consumption patterns here either.

Hansen, like most environmentalists, blames the "special interests" and spineless political leadership for the failure to enact carbon taxes:

> "Today we are faced with the need to achieve rapid reductions in global fossil fuel emissions and to nearly phase out fossil fuel emissions by the end of the century. Most governments are saying they that they recognize these imperatives. And they say they will meet these objectives... Ladies and gentlemen, your governments are lying through their teeth... Moreover, they are now taking actions that, if we do not stop them, will lock in guaranteed failure to achieve the targets that they have nominally accepted... First, they are allowing construction of new coal-fired plants. Second, they are allowing construction of coal-to-liquids plants that will produce oil from coal. Third, they are allowing development of unconventional fossil fuels such as tar sands. Fourth, they are

---

[22] Lizzy Davies, "Humiliation for green convert Sarkozy as carbon tax ruled unconstitutional," the *Guardian*, December 30, 2009.

leasing public lands and remote areas for oil and gas exploration to search for the last drop of hydrocarbons. Fifth, they are allowing companies to lease land for hydraulic fracturing, an environmentally destructive mining technique... to extract every last bit of gas... Sixth, they are allowing highly-destructive mountain-top removal and long-wall mining of coal... And on and on.

"The problem is that our governments, under the heavy thumb of special interests, are not pursuing policies that would restrict our fossil fuel use... Quite the contrary, they are pursuing policies to get every last drop of fossil fuel, including coal, by whatever means necessary, regardless of environmental damage. [And this is despite the fact] that we have all the ingredients we need to meet this challenge – except leadership willing to buck the special financial interests benefiting from business as usual."[23]

But the problem is not just special interests, lobbyists and corruption. Even courageous political leaders could not turn the situation around. Because none of these things are the problem. The problem is capitalism. Because, *given capitalism*, it is, perversely, in the *general interest*, in *everyone's immediate interests* to do all we can to maxmize growth right now, therefore, unavoidably, to maximize fossil fuel consumption right now – because practically every job in the country is, in one way or another, dependent upon fossil fuel consumption. And any cutback, particularly the massive and urgent cuts that climate scientists like Jim Hansen say we have to make to save the humans in the decades and centuries to come, can only come at the expense of massive layoffs for the humans in the here and now. There is no way to cut CO_2 emissions by anything like 80 percent without imposing drastic cuts across the board in industrial production. But since we live under capitalism, not socialism, no one is promising new jobs to all those coal miners, oil drillers, gas frackers, power plant operators, farmers and fertilizer manufacturers, loggers and builders, autobuilders, truck drivers, airplane builders, airline pilots and crews and the countless other occupations whose jobs would be at risk if fossil fuel use were really seriously curtailed.[24] So rational people can understand the science, grasp the

---

[23] *Storms*, pp. 185-86.
[24] For example, Elizabeth Rosenthal, "Grim local choices as Europe goes green," *International Herald Tribune*, September 16, 2010. The EU passed its first law to phase out

implications of the failure to act right now, *and still find they have to "live in denial" to carry on.* Given capitalism, they have little choice but to focus on the short-term, to prioritize saving their jobs in the here and now to feed their kids today – and worry about tomorrow, tomorrow. That's why, when in 2009 President Obama tried to eliminate some tax credits and deductions tied to coal, oil and natural gas, there was furious protest from coal states and congress never enacted the changes. That's why the United Auto Workers (UAW) have often joined their bosses in protesting against Environmental Protection Agency efforts to impose higher CAFE (Corporate Average Fuel Economy) standards. It's not that *personally* those workers don't understand that we all need to consume less oil.[25] But what other choice do they have given that, today, Detroit's best defense against the Asian invasion is to concentrate on its niche market building giant gas-hog Ticonderogas, Escalades, Suburbans, Dodge Ram and Ford F150 trucks? Given capitalism, tragically, the autoworkers' best hope for job security today is to work to destroy their children's tomorrows.

The science vs. the political economy

This is the awful choice workers face in every industry under capitalism. That's why, with the world's leading industrial economies locked in ferocious global competition, especially against China's capitalist police-state advantage, with unemployment levels at 10 percent in the U.S. and Europe, 20 to 40 percent or more for youth, and half the youth population from Mexico to Egypt to India unemployed, the last thing any capitalist government wants to do right now is impose a carbon tax because the first consequence of making fossil fuels more expensive would be to threaten the extremely fragile global "recovery" and compound their already severe unemployment problems, if not actually provoke revolt. And given the state of

---

coal in 2002, especially in the coal-dependent East European states, but deadlines have been repeatedly moved back because, with the transition to capitalism, workers just face unemployment as state job guarantees have been capitalist-rationally eliminated. As one worker told Rosenthal: "After 20 years in the mine, your body is pretty damaged and so you're not so employable."

[25] There have been conspicuous exceptions to this pattern. For example, in the midst of the 2009 recession, a UAW caravan brought UAW workers from Detroit to Washington D.C. to demand that shuttered auto plants be converted to making much-needed mass transit and light rail vehicles, or alternative energy equipment like windmill turbines. See "Auto caravan voices grievances of union autoworkers" by Wendy Thompson, Detroit Green Party and UAW convention delegate, in *Green Pages,* February 5, 2009 at http://gp.org/greenpages-blog/?p=992.

global competition today, with their economies already half de-industrialized, American and European industrialists not unreasonably protest that, why should their industries be so burdened when everyone knows that China is never going to impose any such tax? In today's world, American industrialists would not be wrong to say, like their German counterparts, that at the end of the day, a carbon tax would bring on "the de-industrialilzation of America". And yet even in the best of boom times, when America and Europe ruled the world economy, every president from Ronald Reagan to Bill Clinton to George Bush *père* and *fils* and all their congresses, democratic and republican alike, refused to support legislation that would in any way threaten growth and "the American way of life". In an economy where after more than half a century of efforts, we can't even get a lousy five-cent bottle deposit bill passed in more than a handful of states (nine to be precise), let alone a serious gasoline tax anywhere, why would Paul Hawken imagine that congress would pass a carbon tax that would "drive the coal industry out of business in two decades time"?

II.A.3. The inevitable failure of market solutions

Since no government is going to impose carbon taxes, the entire green tax strategy collapses because, as Hawken, Brown and Cairncross freely admit, profit seeking and environmental protection are irreconcilably opposed. Yet the worst problem with the carbon tax idea is that even if serious carbon taxes were actually imposed, *there is no guarantee whatsoever that they would reduce greenhouse gas emissions* because they would do little if anything to stop overall growth and consumption. That's why, even though in the U.S. calls for green taxes have elicited fierce opposition from many quarters, nevertheless, many in government, many businesses, and a long list of industrial CEOs including Rex Tillerson, CEO of ExxonMobil and Paul Anderson, CEO of Duke Energy, *support* carbon taxes – because they understand that unlike cap and trade, carbon taxes would add something to the cost of doing business, like other taxes, but they pose no finite limit to growth.[26] Worse, because carbon taxes are transparently a tax, most carbon advocates have tendered their proposals as "revenue neutral" to make them more palatable to politicians, business and consumers. Paul Hawken and Al Gore call for "offsetting" carbon taxes by reducing income taxes. Jim Hansen's "tax and dividend" plan proposes "returning 100 percent of the collected tax back to the

---

[26] For the list of CEOs who support carbon taxes, see The Carbon Tax Center at http://www.carbontax.org/who-supports/opinion-leaders/.

public in the form of a dividend."[27] Yet, as ecological economist William E. Rees, co-founder of the science of ecological footprint analysis, points out, if carbon tax offsets are revenue neutral, then they are also "impact neutral". Money returned to consumers will likely just be spent on something else that consumes or trashes the planet. So, says Rees, if a consumer, say, takes an eco-car rebate from the government to junk his/her clunker for a Prius, this could save a several hundred bucks in fuel costs each year. But if the consumer then spends the savings on, say, a round-trip air ticket to some vacation destination (which s/he could do every year with the fuel savings) or buys a new heavily polluting flat-screen TV, the carbon "savings" would evaporate. And, meanwhile, s/he's added more to the global waste heap by junking the clunker. [28] In the end, to coin a phrase, taxing pollution is a problem, not a solution.

Why not just regulate it?

Of course, the government could just drop these market approaches and directly regulate CO_2 output by imposing fixed limits on greenhouse gas emitters, like governments already regulates many toxic chemicals. Legally, President Obama has the authority under clean air legislation to do just that. And since his election, the somewhat emboldened EPA has asserted its right to do so. But where fossil fuels are concerned we're not just talking about banning or restricting a single chemical here or there. If we're talking about 80 percent cuts in CO_2 and other greenhouse emissions, then we're talking about the need to impose huge cuts in everything from farming to fashions – which is why business is fiercely resisting Obama's emboldened EPA.[29]

---

[27] Hawken, above, p. 4. Al Gore, *Our Choice* (Emmaus PA: Rodale Press, 2009), p. 343. Hansen, *Storms*, p. 209.
[28] See William Rees and Mathis Wackernagel, *Our Ecological Footprint: Reducing Human Footprint on the Earth* (Gabriola Island, BC, Canada: New Society Publishers, 1996). See also, Rees, "BC's carbon tax shell game," in *The Tyee* (British Columbia) February 26, 2008 at http://thetyee.ca/Views/2008/02/26/TaxShellGame/.
[29] Louise Radnofsky, "Business groups' target: EPA," *Wall Street Journal*, February 7, 2011. And, predictably: "E.P.A. delays tougher rules on emissions," John M Broder and Sheryl Gay Stolberg, *New York Times*, December 10, 2010.

II.B. The economics vs. the science on the scope of the problem

When climate scientists like Jim Hansen tell us we need to "shut down the coal industry" and "leave most of the fossil fuels in the ground" in order to reduce greenhouse gas emissions, it's only natural that, like those autoworkers, *none of us really want to think about the full implications of this imperative.* So the tendency is often to think about this issue in isolation from the rest of economy, as if fossil fuels are just in the "energy sector", which we could fix by switching to renewables, by junking the clunker for a Prius, and go on driving and consuming as before while, hopefully, the economy also keeps on growing. But this is a delusion because in our economy, fossil fuels are in *virtually everything* we depend upon. Today, approximately half of the fossil fuels we extract are burned directly to produce energy in power plants and to propel our vehicles. The other half goes into everything we consume. We literally *eat* fossil fuels at every meal because most of our food is grown with synthetic fertilizers derived from natural gas. We cook with gas. Much of our clothing is made from fossil-fuel-derived fibers. Our buildings are built with hundreds of fossil fuel products from plastic wire coatings to paints. Our entire transportation network not only runs on fossil fuels, but also the cars, truck, ship, planes and trains embody fossil fuels, in one form or another, in virtually every component. Our schools, factories, offices, our phones, computers, TVs, the internet, virtually everything we depend upon consumes fossil fuels. And we use gargantuan quantities of the stuff. Right now, when we add up the coal, oil and the natural gas, the world is consuming some 200 million barrel equivalents of oil every day. That's equal to more than 23 times the daily output of Saudi Arabia, the world's largest producer.[30] Currently, renewables like solar and wind (but excluding nuclear and hydroelectric) provide a grand total of about 0.6 percent of global energy consumption. In short, "getting off fossil fuels" is going to be a challenge, and require big changes – to say the least.

But you would hardly get that impression from listening to the optimistic "green is good for business" scenarios of mainstream economists. Thus the UK's Nicolas Stern, former World Bank Chief Economist and author the *Stern Review,* commissioned by the UK government, says we can prevent runaway global warming by pricing in carbon mitigation and that the cost to do so will only reduce growth by

---

[30] Robert Bryce, *Power Hungry* (New York: Public Affairs, 2010), p. 75.

as little as 1 to 3 percent of GDP per year by 2050.[31] Paul Krugman, echoing Stern and citing figures from a Congressional Budget Office survey of models concludes that "strong climate-change policy would leave the American economy between 1.1 percent and 3.4 percent smaller in 2050 than it would be otherwise." So the whole process, they reassure us, will be fairly painless. Green tech will save us and growth can spiral on ever upward, if only a bit slower.[32] Best-selling *New York Times* columnist Thomas Friedman, cheerleader for globalization and author of *Hot, Flat and Crowded* (2008) claims that if we transition to solar and other renewable energies, then we can even *increase* growth, turn clean energy into a "new growth driver" and produce all the consumer goodies that the billions of Chinese, Indians and the rest of the world could want, so the whole planet can enjoy "the American Way of Life".

Cooking the climate numbers to support GDP growth

The science, however, shows us the lie in such optimistic scenarios. Stern's *Review* has been criticized on many grounds, not least for overestimating the mitigation potentials of renewables and underestimating rising future demands in a misguided effort to support perpetual growth when the science clearly demonstrates that perpetual growth is unsustainable.[33] For a start, when the *Stern Review* claims that the cost of reducing greenhouse gas emissions to three-quarters of current levels will cost around $1 trillion or roughly -1.0 percent of GDP in that year, *it says this is to reduce CO_2 emissions to 550 ppm (which would stabilize global temperatures at around 3°C (5.4°F) above pre-industrial levels).[34]* But no credible climate scientists call for holding emissions at 550 ppm/3°. Climate scientists, including the IPCC, have been strenuously lobbying governments to do everything possible to keep CO_2 emissions *below 400 ppm (with 450 ppm the absolute maximum)*, while Jim Hansen

---

[31] Stern, *The Economics of Climate Change: the Stern Review* (Cambridge: CUP, 2006), chapter 9.

[32] Paul Krugman, "Green economics," *New York Times Magazine*, April 11, 2010, p. 39.

[33] See, for example, Ted Trainer, "A short critique of the Stern Review," *real-world economics review*, issue no. 45, March 2008, at http://www.paecon.net/PAEReview/issue45/Trainer45.pdf. Yet Stern has also been criticized for proposing any GDP cut at all: Frank Ackerman, "Debating climate economics: the Stern Review vs. its critics," Report to the Friends of the Earth England, Wales and Northern Ireland, July 2007 at http://sei-us.org/Publications_PDF/SEI-FOE-DebatingClimateEcon-07.pdf.

[34] Stern, *op cit.*, pp. 227, 234, 239, 260.

and his colleagues at NASA's Goddard Institute have even gone further and argued for pushing them back *below 350 ppm*, because climate scientists fear that once if they climb into the 400s, this could set off all sorts of positive feedback loops, breaching critical tipping points that could accelerate global warming by releasing the huge quantities of methane currently entrapped in the frozen tundra of Siberia and in the methane hydrates at the bottom of the Arctic Ocean, with catastrophic implications for humans and most other species. In his powerful new book, *Storms of My Grandchildren*, Jim Hansen, generally considered the world's pre-eminent climate scientist, writes that the speed of climate change, especially the speed of temperature increase in relation to CO_2 ppm levels, and the shocking speed of Arctic and Antarctic melting, has taken even climate scientists by surprise such that they have had to their revise worst-case scenarios of only a few years ago, in 2007. Whereas as scientists used to think that we could tolerate warming up to 2°C without too much damage:

> "Unfortunately, what has since become clear is that a 2-degree Celsius global warming, or even a 1.7 degree warming, is a disaster scenario."

Hansen now believes that we have to have "a carbon dioxide target of no more than 350 ppm" in order to avoid ice sheet disintegration, massive species extinction, loss of mountain glaciers and fresh water supplies, expansion of the subtropics, increasingly extreme forest fires and floods, and destruction of the great biodiversity of coral reefs.[35] CO_2 levels of 400 or 450 ppm will drive temperatures to 2 or 3 degrees warmer than today. That is not a world we want to see:

> "[T]he last time the Earth was 2 or 3 degrees warmer than today, which means the Middle Pliocene, about three million years ago, it was a rather different planet. Sea level was about 25 meters (80 feet) higher than today. Florida was under water. About a billion people now live at elevations less than 25 meters. It may take a long time for such large a sea level rise to be completed – but if we are foolish enough to start the planet down that road, ice sheet disintegration likely will continue out of our control."[36]

---

[35] *Storms*, pp. 142, 164-165, 180.
[36] *Ibid.*, p. 141.

Green capitalism: the god that failed

Given the enormous dangers that such a high target implies, critics have asked why Stern is so reluctant to aim for a safer target. Marxist ecologist John Bellamy Foster and his colleagues suggest that the answer is to be found in Stern's economics, not the science:

> "The *Stern Review* is very explicit, however, that such a radical mitigation of the problem *should not be attempted.* The costs to the world economy of ensuring that atmospheric CO_2e stabilized at present levels or below would be prohibitive, destabilizing capitalism itself. Paths requiring very rapid emissions cuts, we are told, are unlikely to be economically viable. If global greenhouse gas emissions peaked in 2010, the annual emissions reduction rate necessary to stabilize CO_2e at 450 ppm, the *Stern Review* suggests, would be 7 percent, with emissions dropping by about 70 percent below 2005 levels by 2050. This is viewed as economically insupportable."[37]

Stern asserted that "the world does not have to choose between averting climate change and promoting growth and development."[38] But if the science is right that we need to keep emissions below 400 ppm, or even get them back below 350 ppm, then we would indeed have to make radically deeper cuts in GDP levels than Stern advises, deeper even than the -7 percent per year Stern calculates would be necessary just to get us down to 450 ppm. Since, under capitalism, a contraction of economic output on anything like that scale would mean economic collapse and depression, it is difficult to see how we can make the reductions in greenhouse gasses we have to make to avoid climate catastrophe unless we abandon capitalism. That's the dilemma. So far, most scientists have tended to avoid getting into the contentious economic side of the question. But with respect to the issue of growth, the science is unequivocal: never-ending growth means the end of civilization, if not humanity itself – and in the not-so-far distant future. For a summary of the peer-reviewed science on this subject, read a few chapters of Mark Lynas' harrowing *Six Degrees.*[39]

---

[37] John Bellamy Foster, Brett Clark and Richard York, *The Ecological Rift* (New York: Monthly Review Press, 2011), p. 155 and the sources cited therein. Their powerful critique should be read in its entirety. .
[38] Stern, *op cit.*, p. xvii.
[39] *Six Degrees* (Washington D.C.: National Geographic Society, 2008).

Green capitalism: the god that failed

Global warming is surely the most urgent threat we face, but it is far from the only driver of global ecological collapse. Even if we switched to clean renewable electric power tomorrow, this would not stop the overconsumption of forests, fish, minerals and fresh water. It would not stop pollution, or solve the garbage crisis, or stop the changes in ocean chemistry. Indeed, the advent of cheap, clean energy could even *accelerate* these trends.[40] Numerous credible scientific and environmental researchers back up what the climate scientists have been telling us, to demonstrate why perpetual growth is the road to collective social suicide. The following is an example.

In 2005 the **United Nations Millennium Ecosystem Assessment** team of 1300 scientists from 95 countries issued a landmark report on humanity's overconsumption of "natures' services". The scientists reported that 60% (15 out of 24) of the ecosystems examined that are critical for human survival are being "degraded or used unsustainably" including fresh water, capture fisheries, coral reefs, wetlands, drylands and forests. Around the world, many of these are on the verge of collapse. Thus nature's ability to provide the resources for growing future populations is very much in doubt unless radical steps are taken very soon. The report concluded, among other things, that to keep planet-wide temperatures from rising more than two degrees Celsius (the threshold beyond which climatologists think runaway heating will occur), requires that anthropogenic carbon emissions start declining by no later than 2015 and level off at 800 to 1,800 pounds per year per person by 2050.[41] Americans currently generate about 12,000 pounds of CO_2 emissions per person per year and, as the Chinese pointedly told Obama at Copenhagen in 2009, Americans have no "right" to produce emissions at more than world per capita average, even less any right to demand that others cut emissions if we do not sharply reduce our own emissions. This means that for Americans to pollute our "fair share" *we will have to slash our use of fossil fuels by something on the order of 80-90% by 2050*, 40 years from now. One can quibble that it's difficult to cut back so drastically and so quickly when our economy has been built on fossil fuels and high level consumption, whereas the modernizing Chinese do not need to recreate, for example, the horrors of Los Angeles traffic and pollution all over again.

---

[40] On this see my "Beyond growth or beyond capitalism," *real-world economics review*, no. 53, May 2010, pp. 28-42.

[41] *Millennium Ecosystem Assessment, Synthesis Report* (New York: United Nations, 2005), available at http://www.maweb.org/documents/document.356.aspx.pdf.

Be that as it may, if we do not make a huge effort to cut back, no one else will either, in which case, our collective goose is cooked.

In its 2008 *Living Planet Report*, the World Wide Fund for Nature (WWF) similarly concluded that people are plundering the world's resources at a rate that far outstrips the planet's capacity to sustain life. The planet's 7+ billion people are currently consuming 20 percent more natural resources per year than can be reproduced by natural regeneration (and many resources, like oil, cannot be replenished at all). The report noted that global populations of terrestrial, freshwater and marine species fell on average by 40 percent between 1970 and 2000 due to destruction of natural habitats, pollution, overfishing and other anthropogenic causes. More than three quarters of the world's people live in nations where national consumption has outstripped their country's biological capacity. James Leape, Director General of WWF, says that, "Most of us are propping up our current lifestyles, and our economic growth, by drawing – and increasingly overdrawing – on the ecological capital of other parts of the world. If our demands on the planet continue to increase at the same rate, by the mid-2030s we would need the equivalent of two planets to maintain our lifestyles."[42]   This is to say, a rather different conclusion about the implication of endless growth than that drawn by Krugman, Stern and Friedman.

And in its own *2010 State of the World Report* the World Watch Institute says that:

> "As consumerism has taken root in culture upon culture over the past half-century, it has become a powerful driver of the inexorable increase in demand for resources and production of waste that marks our age. . . More than 6.8 billion human beings are now demanding ever greater quantities of material resources, decimating the world's richest ecosystems, and dumping billions of tons of heat-trapping gases into the atmosphere each year. Despite a 30-percent increase in resource efficiency, global resource use has expanded 50 percent over the past three decades. And those numbers could continue to soar for decades to come as more than 5 billion people who currently consume one tenth as

---

[42] WWF, "Living Planet analysis shows looming ecological crunch," posted 29 October 2008 at http://wwf.panda.org/wwf_news/news/?uNewsID=148922.

many resources per person as the average European try to follow the trail blazed by the world's affluent."[43]

In short, as Erik Assadourian, the lead author concludes:

> "...the American or even the European way of life is simply not viable... Add to this fact that population is projected to grow by another 2.3 billion by 2050 and... it becomes clear that while shifting technologies and stabilizing population will be essential in creating sustainable societies, neither will succeed without considerable changes in consumption patterns, *including reducing and even eliminating the use of certain goods, such as cars and airplanes, that have become important parts of life today for many.*[44]

Got four more planets?

So the world's leading scientists, scientific bodies and environmental think tanks have warned us not only that growth just can't go on, but also that, at least in the industrialized economies, *we have to stop and go into reverse.* This is a message not many of us really want to hear despite the benefits of such sacrifices – like our children's survival. But if the science is right, we don't have much choice. Either we completely transform our economic system or we face the collapse of civilization. It's that simple. But of course the problem is, as always, how can we "cut back" under capitalism?

II.C. Natural limits to "greening" any economy

Green capitalism proponents often take it as an article of faith that technological breakthroughs will enable us to sharply cut resource use, to "dematerialize" production and, in the words of the *Stern Review*, to "decouple growth from greenhouse gas emissions" such that production can grow forever while resource consumption declines.[45] While no doubt there are many green technological miracles on the horizon, they cannot save us so long as we live in a capitalist economy.

---

[43] *State of the World 2010*, (New York: Norton, 2010) pp. xvii-xviii.
[44] *State of the World 2010*, pp. 6-7 (my italics).
[45] Elaborated most fully in *Natural Capitalism*. See also Stern, *op cit.*, p. xvii.

That's because, first, as noted above, under capitalism, there is no assurance that greater energy efficiency or materialist conservation would mean less consumption or less pollution *so long as there is no extra market limit set to the growth of overall production*. Efficiency gains could just as easily enable producers to use saved resources to expand production even more instead of "saving" resources. And, given capitalism, there is every incentive to do just that and every penalty for failing to do so. Secondly, the prospects for "dematerialization" are extremely limited, often completely impossible, outside of a very few industries. Thirdly, in many instances where companies actually adopt clean production technologies or waste minimization, such "green practices" are beside the point since the main cause of pollution are the products the company produces, such as toxic pesticides, not the process of producing them. And fourthly, "green" industries very often just create new problems in the place of old. Taking the last first:

II.C.1. Certified organic: green gone wrong

Many "green" start-ups have found that it's hard to go green in the real world. Even when it's theoretically possible to shift to greener production, given capitalism, as often as not, "green" industries just replace old problems with new problems. So burning down tracts of the Amazon rainforest in order to plant sugarcane to produce organic sugar for Whole Foods or ethanol to feed cars instead of people, is not so green after all. Neither is burning down Indonesian and Malaysian rainforests to plant palm-oil plantations so Britons can tool around London in their obese Landrovers. But such examples are what Heather Rogers calls "green gone wrong" instead of the "win-win" solutions touted by pro-market environmentalists just a few years ago.[46] Aquaculture was supposed to save wild fish. But this turns out to be just another case of "green gone wrong" because, aside from contaminating farmed fish (and fish eaters) with antibiotics to suppress disease in fish pens, most farm-raised fish are carnivores. Feeding ever-more farmed fish requires capturing ever-more wild forage fish to grind up for fishmeal for the farm-raised fish which leaves ever-fewer fish in the ocean, starving those up the food chain like sharks, seals, dolphins and whales. So instead of saving wild fish, fish farming has actually *accelerated* the plunder of the last remaining stocks of wild fish in the oceans.[47]   "Green

---

[46] Heather Rogers, *Green Gone Wrong* (New York: Scribner, 2010).
[47] Daniel Pauly, et al., "Fishing down marine food webs" *Science,* 279, 1998 pp. 860-863. Nancy Baron, "Global appetite for farmed fish devouring world's wild fish supplies," *Environmental News Nework,* February 19, 2001. Rosamond L. Naylor, et al., "Feeding

certification" schemes were supposed to reduce tropical deforestation by shaming Home Depot and similar big vendors into sourcing their wood and pulp from "certified" "sustainable" forests – the "sustainable" part is that these "forests" get replanted. But such wood "plantations" are never planted on land that was previously unforested. Instead, they just replace natural forest. There's nothing sustainable about burning down huge tracts of native Indonesian or Amazonian tropical forests, killing off or running off all the wild animals and indigeneous people that lived there, in order to plant sterile eucalyptus plantations to harvest pulp for paper. To make matters worse, market demand from overconsuming, but guilt-ridden Americans and Europeans has forced green certifiers to lower their standards so much to keep up with demand such that, today, in most cases, ecological "certification" is virtually meaningless.

For example, the Forestry Stewardship Council (FSC), the largest such organization, has come under fire for allowing its tree-with-checkmark logo to be used by rainforest-raping lumber and paper companies, for taking the word of auditors paid by the companies, for loosening its standards to allow just 50% certified pulp to go into paper making. The problem is that *the FSC is not an international government body with a universal mandate and authority to certify the world's lumber.* It's just a self-funding NGO environmental organization like the NRDC or the WWF or Greenpeace. Such organizations live on voluntary contributions from supporters, on contributions from corporate funders, and/or on payment for services. As these organizations grew in size and ambition, they sought bigger budgets to better fufill their "missions" – more than they could solicit from individual contributors. With few exceptions, nearly all these organizations eventually adopted "business" models that drove them into the arms of corporate contributors, in this case, typically lumber companies. In the case of the FSC, when it was founded in 1993 it certified just three producers whose lumber was 100 percent sustainable and not many more in the following years. But by 1997, as the organization faced competition from new "entrants" into the green product-labeling "field" (to use capitalist lingo), the FSC faced the problem, as the *Wall Street Journal* reported, of "how to maintain high standards while promoting their logos and increasing the supply of approved products to meet demand from consumers and big retailers". This is ever the contradiction in our capitalist world. In the end, "green" lumber certification, like so many other nominally "green" NGOs has steadily drifted away from its mission and

Aquaculture in an Era of Finite Resources" *Proceedings of the National Academy of Sciences*, Vol. 106 no. 36, pp. 1503-15110.

become more and more co-partners in corporate plunder of world's remaining forests.[48]

II.C.2. Fantasies of de-coupling and dematerialization

In the 1980s and 90s eco-futurists like Paul Hawken and Amory Lovins predicted that big technological fixes would make it possible to "de-link" or "de-couple" growth from pollution. Nicolas Stern makes the same claim in his 2006 *Stern Review*.[49] Some governments and industries tried. For example, in the 1990s, the British government under Tony Blair, born-again environmentalist, tried to get serious about climate change. Parliament passed a major climate-change bill in 2007 that mandated a 26 percent reduction below 1990 levels of greenhouse gases by 2020, and 60 percent cut by 2050. But as Boston economist Juliet Schor reports, so far "the British approach is failing and dramatically so". That's because, while calling for emissions reductions, the Labour government was also:

> "... *adamant about growth*, arguing that efficiency, clean energy,
> and a market for carbon will do the trick. The government thought
> that it could 'decarbonize', or sever the link between emissions
> and GDP."[50]

So the environment ministry enacted programs to reduce food waste, plastics consumption and other measures to reduce the "carbon footprint". But to no avail. U.K. CO_2 emissions actually fell during the 2008-09 recession and the U.K was one of the only European successful cases under the first round of the Kyoto agreements. But virtually all those reductions came from phasing out coal, which has been displaced by North Sea oil, and all agree that this gain can't last once the oil runs out. During the Blair period from 1997-2006, despite government efforts, CO_2 emissions actually rose. As Schor says:

> "Refusal to reconsider their stance on growth has doomed efforts
> to meet even the now scientifically inadequate targets of the 2007

---

[48] See Tom Wright and Jim Carlton, "FSC's 'green' label companies cut virgin forest," *Wall Street Journal*, October 30, 2007. More generally, see also, *Green, Inc.* (Guilford Conn.: The Lyons Press, 2008).
[49] *Stern Review*, p. xvii and chapter 16.
[50] *Plenitude*, p. 91, my italics.

bill. Projected growth in one sector alone, aviation, will likely account for the entire country's carbon budget in 2050."

And, as Schor further describes, "de-linking" has fared even worse in the United States:

"Since 1975, the U.S. has made substantial progress in improving energy efficiency. Energy expended per dollar of GDP has been cut in half. But rather than falling, energy demand has increased, by roughly 40 percent. Moreover, demand is rising fastest in those sectors that have had the biggest efficiency gains – transport and residential energy use. Refrigerator efficiency improved by 10 percent but the number of refrigerators in use rose 20 percent. In aviation, fuel consumption per mile fell by more than 40 percent, but total fuel use grew by 150 percent because passenger miles rose. Vehicles are a similar story. And with soaring demand, we've had soaring emissions. Carbon dioxide from these two sectors has risen 40 percent, twice the rate of the larger economy."[51]

So time and again, growth outstrips efficiency gains. It almost seems like a law of nature: making more stuff uses more stuff. Who'd have thunk it?

II.C.3. The electric/hybrid car solution to what?

In the same way, green tech enthusiasts like Amory Lovins have argued that huge efficiency gains, super-light materials, hybrid-electric propulsion systems and whatnot could revolutionize auto transportation and clear the air. But as Lovins himself points out, the advent of his hypercars could just as easily "worsen traffic and road congestion by making driving even cheaper and more attractive". Because that's exactly what's happened with every other advance: "The fuel saved by the 1980s doubling of U.S. new-car efficiency was promptly offset by the greater number of cars and more driving... Global car registrations have been growing more than twice as fast as the population – 50 million cars in 1954, 350 million in 1989, 500 million in 1997."[52] And they're growing even faster now that China has become

---

[51] *Ibid.*, pp. 89-90, 92, my italics.
[52] Hawken, *Natural Capitalism*, p. 40.

the world's biggest car market. So we cannot assume that even the advent of super fuel-efficient cars would lessen pollution *if there is no extra-market limit on the number of automobiles produced.*

To make matters worse, vehicle pollution is not confined to what comes out of the tailpipe. A life-cycle study of the automobile carried out by the Umwelt-und Prognose-Institut of Heidelberg Germany in 1993, found that only 40 percent of an average car's pollution is emitted during the car's "driving" life stage. The other 60 percent results from other life stages: the extraction of raw materials, the transport of raw materials, the manufacturing of the car and the disposal of the car. Most of the pollution any car will ever produce – 56 percent – is generated in the manufacturing process before the car even arrives at the showroom, i.e. in the production of all the steel, aluminum, copper and other metals, glass, rubber, plastic, paint and other resources that go into every automobile, and in the manufacturing process itself. Cars produce 56 percent of all the pollution they will ever produce *before they ever hit the road*, and 4 percent after they are retired and junked. So even if automakers could produce dramatically lighter and more fuel efficient cars, so long as they are free to produce automobiles without limit, more cars will just mean more pollution, even if they're hybrids or plug-in electric cars.[53]

Those coal-powered cars of the future

To further confound green hopes for an electric car tech fix, it turns out that electric cars could be even be *more polluting* than the current generation of gasoline-powered cars. That's because electric cars are only as clean as the fuel used to produce the electricity they run on. And in the real world, plug-in electric cars are in most countries largely *coal-powered cars* and likely to become increasingly so. Thus, paradoxically, in the real world of today, gasoline-powered cars produce fewer emissions than electric cars. Scientists at Oxford University recently modeled projected emissions from battery electric vehicles given different power generation mixes and concluded that if countries like India and China powered their automobilization booms with battery electric vehicles, this would be actually produce more CO_2 emissions than if they did so with conventional petroleum

---

[53] See John Whitelegg, "Dirty From Cradle to Grave," (1993) a translated summary of the German study. Available at http://www.worldcarfree.net/resources/free.php

powered vehicles.[54] That's because coal is the dirtiest of fossil fuels, far dirtier than gasoline, but according to the International Energy Agency (IEA), the share of coal used for global electricity generation is likely to increase. According to the IEA, in 2006, coal comprised 41 percent of electricity-generation fuel; natural gas 20 percent; hydropower 16 percent; nuclear 15 percent; and "other" (including renewables) 2 percent. By 2030 the IEA predicts that coal's share will rise to 44 percent of electricity generation, gas will account for 20 percent, hydropower 14 percent, nuclear 10 percent, with "other" rising only to 9 percent.[55] And since oil is slated to run out long before coal, coal's share could rise still further. So electricity generation is still likely to remain a very dirty business for a long time, and indeed, the share of electricity generated by the dirtiest fuel, coal, is likely to increase.

Finally, if we turn to the actual production of electric vehicles, it turns out that this process is heavily polluting as well. That's because producing those endless nickel and lithium batteries, mining the iron and copper and rare earths that go into the motors and controls, not to mention the as-yet-barely-discussed problem of what to do with all the millions and eventually billions of large, toxic, worn out batteries that have to end up somewhere, creates somewhat different resource consumption and pollution problems from those of gasoline and diesel engines, but by no means fewer problems.[56] For example, each of the one million Priuses that Toyota sells in the United States has a battery that contains 32 pounds of nickel. Just the production of that one car, at current rates, is said to consume fully 1 percent of all the world's annually produced nickel. And the mining and smelting of nickel is one of the most polluting of all industrial operations. Norilsk Nickel, a Russian company in northern Siberia, is the world's largest producer of nickel and largest smelter of heavy metals. According to WorstPolluted.org, Norilsk ranks no. seven of the 10 most polluted industrial sites on the planet. The city (founded as a slave labor camp under Stalin), where the snow is black, the air tastes of sulphur and the life expectancy of workers is 10 years less than the Russian average, is one of the most unhealthy places in an unhealthy country. Production at that plant has poisoned the soil for 60 kilometers around the plant, local adults and children suffer from numerous respiratory

---

[54] Reed T. Doucette and Malcom D. McCulloch, "Modeling the CO_2 emissions from battery electric vehicles given the power generation mixes of different countries," *Energy Policy* 39.2, February 2011, pp. 803-811.
[55] These figures are quoted in Robert Bryce, *Power Hungry* (New York: Public Affairs, 2010), p. 58 Figure 5.
[56] Don Sherman, "When electric-car batteries die, where will they end up?" *New York Times,* June 13, 2010.

diseases, cancer, etc.[57] A Norwegian government study reports that Norilsk's SO_2 emissions (2,000,000 tons a year) produce acid rain around the Arctic circle. The company also discharges large amounts of copper, nickel, as well as cobalt, vanadium and other metals into freshwater lakes, streams and much ends up in the Arctic Sea.[58] And that's just the nickel. Lithium mining is another nightmare.[59] And then there's the 'rare earths' nightmare.[60]

In short, efforts to decrease air pollution by getting "old, polluting" cars off the road to only replace them with new, "cleaner" cars can be misguided because such efforts have typically focused on pollution emitted solely during the driving stage and thus have missed 60 percent of the problem, and also because they have tended to overlook the pollution resulting from electricity generation. Seen in this light, I would not be surprised if the most ecological and efficient cars on the planet today are not those Toyota Priuses or Chevy Volts with their estimated 7-10 lifespan, but those ancient Chevrolets, Oldsmobiles and Fords cruising around the streets of Havana. For even if their gas mileage is lower than auto producer fleet averages today, they were still only produced *once*, whereas American "consumers" have gone through an average of seven generations of cars since then, with all the manufacturing and disposal pollution that entailed. Surely an ecological society has to come up with cars (gas or electric or whatever) that that can be rebuilt, reused, upgraded, and completely recycled when it's most rational to do so instead of just crushed every few years so new ones can be sold.

---

[57] "Top 10 Most Polluted Places, 2007," at
http://www.worstpolluted.org/projects_reports/display/43.
[58] "To the Ministry of Finance, Recommendation of 16 February 2009" by the Council on Ethics, Norwegian Government Pension Fund (2009) at
http://www.regjeringen.no/upload/FIN/Statens%20pensjonsfond/recommendation_norilsk.pdf
[59] See, for example, the excellent report by Dan McDougal: "In search of Lithium: the battle for the third element," *Daily Mail Online* (London) April 5, 2009 at http://www.dailymail.co.uk/home/moslive/article-1166387/In-search-Lithium-The-battle-3rd-element.html. Also, Damian Kahya, "Bolivia holds key to electric car," *BBC News Online*, November 9, 2008 at http://news.bbc.co.uk/2/hi/7707847.stm.
[60] Keith Bradsher, "A new reckoning on costs of rare earths," *New York Times*, November 1, 2010; and idem, "In China, illegal rare earth mines face crackdown," *New York Times*, December 29, 2010.

II.C.4. The clean, green energy solution to what?

Energy generation is probably the one field where there are substantial possibilities for green capitalism. The prospect of "clean green energy" – solar, wind and other renewable – is everybody's favorite green tech innovation. Shifting most electricity generation to solar, wind and other renewables could radically dematerialize this sector and reduce the largest single demand for coal (as well as oil and natural gas) and so could, in principle, dramatically reduce CO_2 pollution, acid rain and also bring wide health benefits. But, the first problem with this tech fix is that it's difficult to produce "base-load" power – consistent 24/7 power generation – with renewables.[61] Sunlight, wind and water flow are all variable and unpredictable. But trainloads of coal and oil can normally be depended upon.[62] Renewable energy scientists maintain that integrated comprehensive systems can solve the problem of base-load generation. The IEA estimates that solar power alone could produce almost a quarter of the world's electricity needs by 2050.[63] But others, like Jim Hansen and James Lovelock, have called for a radical shift to nuclear power as the only way to get 24/7 power in the near future. But of course nuclear reactors pose a different set of problems. For a start, there is the virtually inevitable threat of accidents somewhere, sometime. Then there is the as-yet-unsolved problem of what to do with all the spent fuel. But in addition, it is also not clear that uranium fuel is any less an inexhaustible resource than oil was once thought to be. And the potential tech fix for the tech fix – the thesis that "next generation" "fast" nuclear reactors could recycle their own fuel or run on spent fuel, has a certain familiar "too-cheap-to-meter" ring to it, but remains for the moment hypothetical, and in any event, will certainly be a hugely expensive and dangerous way to boil water.[64]

---

[61] On this see Hansen, *Storms,* chapter 9.

[62] Clifford Krauss, "There will be fuel," *New York Times*, November 17, 2010.

[63] Joel Kirkland, "IEA: Solar power could produce nearly one-quarter of global electricity by 2050," *Scientific American,* May 12, 2010 at
http://www.scientificamerican.com/article.cfm?id=solar-power-global-electricity.   Also:
"Beyond fossil fuels: David Mills on solar power," interview in *Scientific American*, April 28, 2009, at
http://www.scientificamerican.com/article.cfm?id=energy-mills-ausra.

[64] See the options discussed in "The Future of the Nuclear Cycle, an Interdisciplinary MIT Study" published in Septermber 2010 and available at
http://web.mit.edu/mitei/docs/spotlights/nuclear-fuel-cycle.pdf. Also, Hansen, *op cit*. pp. 194-204.

Secondly, even if a shift to renewables could provide us with relatively unlimited supplies of clean electricity, we can't assume that this would necessarily lead to massive permanent reductions in pollution. That's because, on the Jevons principle I discussed elsewhere, *if there are no non-market constraints on production,* then the advent of cheap clean energy production could just give a huge (if solar powered) green light to the manufacturers of endless electric vehicles, appliances, lighting, laptops, phones, iPads and new toys we can't even imagine yet.[65] But the expanded production all this stuff, on a global scale, would just consume ever more raw materials, more metals, petrochemicals, rare earths, etc. , produce more and more pollution, destroy more and more of the environment, and all end up in some landfill somewhere someday. In sum, it would appear that, at the end of the day, *the only way society can really put the brakes on overconsumption of electricity is to impose non-market limits on electricity production and consumption, enforce radical conservation, and stop making all the unnecessary gadgets that demand endless supplies of power.*

II.C.5. Green resource extraction?

And energy generation is actually one of the very few industries where dematerialization is seriously possible on a significant scale. For most of the economy, there are few possibilities of dematerialization at all. Start with resource extraction. Virtually everything we consume starts with primary extraction of raw materials – oil, natural gas, minerals, lumber, food, fiber and oil crops, fresh water and so on – which are either consumed directly or become the basis of further processing and manufacturing. But logging can't be "dematerialized". Fishing can't be dematerialized. Farming can't be dematerialized. Drilling for oil and gas are polluting industries. Same with refining. Accidents happen. Regularly.[66] Hydraulic "fracking" poisons water supplies.[67] There is just no way to extract metals from their ores in any way that "mimics nature". It's just a "linear" process. And I am still trying to figure out how chopping and burning down Javanese rainforests and replacing them with "teak plantations" to furnish so-called "sustainably harvested

---

[65] "Beyond Growth" in *op cit.*

[66] Tom Knudson, "Quest for oil leaves trail of damage across the globe," *McClatchy Newspapers*, May 16, 2010, at www.quest-for-oil-leaves-trail-of.html. Joe Brock, "Africa's oil spills are far from U.S. media glare," *Reuters*, May 19, 2010, at http://www.commondreams.org/headline/2010/05/19-3.

[67] Kirk Johnsom, "E.P.A. links tainted water in Wyoming to hydraulic fracturing for natural gas," *New York Times*, December 9, 2011.

wood" for the signature "Teak for Life" lawn furniture that Smith & Hawken flogs to American suburbanites, squares with Paul Hawken's notion of a "restorative economy".[68] Destruction and pollution from primary resource extraction is growing exponentially both because global demand is surging as capitalist development produces more and more "consumers" in the industrializing world, and because the easily accessible resources are often tapped out. American mainland oil fields were exhausted decades ago. Coastal shallow-water oil fields in the Gulf of Mexico are running out. So the oil companies have to go further offshore, taking on additional risks to drill in deep water.[69] They have to turn to tar sands in Canada and Venezuela which are both heavily polluting and energy intensive to develop. And gas drillers have had to turn to "fracking" to reach deeper gas supplies in the United States. These are all dirty, dangerous and risky methods of production and there is no practical way to make them much cleaner. "Clean coal" is a fraud perpetrated by the coal industry without a shred of evidence for practical possibilities on an industrial scale.[70] But coal is not only burned to generate electricity (a "bad" for Paul Hawken), coal is critical for making steel, and coal provides carbon for aluminum smelting. And coal and coal by-products are critical for paper making and many other products from rayon and nylon to specialist products like carbon fiber, carbon filters, etc. So no coal, no steel or aluminum. No steel and aluminum, no windmills or solar panels or high speed trains ("goods"). No coal, no carbon fiber no superlight "hyper cars". So "taxing coal out of business" would undermine some of Paul Hawken's other environmental goals. Same with oil. Oil and oil by-products are indispensable for petrochemicals, plastics, plastic film for solar panels, plastic insulation for electric wires and countless thousands of other products. Oil is so critical for so many industrial products and processes that it is just inconceivable to imagine a modern industrial civilization without oil. Rare earths mining is no less a dirty process. But no rare earths, no windmill generators, no electric cars, no cell phones or iPads. And the search for lithium to make the batteries for all those future

---

[68] Smith & Hawken, *Teak For Life* (Summer 1999 catalogue), wood source noted on p. 6.
[69] Jad Mouawad and Barry Meier, "Risk-taking rises to new levels as oil rigs in Gulf drill deeper," August 30, 2010. Russell Gold, "Exxon dives deep into high-risk exploration," *Wall Street Journal*, February 2, 2010. Guy Chazan, "BP taps deep water to grow," *Wall Street Journal*, March 12, 2010. Clifford Krauss, "Accidents don't slow Gulf of Mexico drilling," *New York Times*, April 23, 2010.
[70] See Hansen's demolition of the "clean coal" propaganda in his *Storms of My Grandchildren*, pp. 174ff.

electric cars threatens fragile ecologies from Bolivia to Finland, Mexico to Canada.[71]

Metals smelting is, likewise, an extremely polluting process with little real potential for greening which is why producers have "cleaned up pollution" in the U.S. by shipping it overseas when possible, out of reach of U.S. and European environmental laws.[72] But no copper means no electric lines from those solar panels and no electric motors for those windmills and electric cars. No aluminium means no windmill generators or light vehicles. Lester Brown actually argued that we could dramatically reduce, even almost stop producing some metals, like steel and aluminum, because these metals are, in principle, endlessly recyclable. So he wrote that:

> "Advanced industrial economies will come to rely primarily on the stock of materials already in the economy rather than on virgin raw materials. For metals such as steel and aluminum, the losses through use will be minimal. With the appropriate policies, metal – once it is invested in the economy – can be used indefinitely."[73]

This is a perfect example of the unreal, other-worldly, a-historical thinking that is rife in eco-futurist writing. How could we ever do this in a capitalist economy? Are Toyota or General Motors looking to produce the same number of steel cars next year as this year? Is Airbus Industries looking to sell the same number of aluminum airplanes in the next decade as in this decade? To ask the question is to answer it. Is Suntech, China's largest manufacturer of solar panels, planning to manufacture the same number of steel and aluminum-framed solar panels next year as it made this year? Well, actually, I imagine Lester Brown would want Suntech to make *more* panels next year – a lot more. But *there will be environmental costs to that*, of course. Many metals are recyclable, but world demand for aluminum, copper, steel, nickel and other metals, not to mention "rare earths" is soaring as more and more of the world modernizes and industrializes. That's why resource-starved China is buying up the world, snapping up Australian coal mines, Afghani and Peruvian copper mines, Indonesian forests, Mozambique farmland and more to feed its huge and rapidly growing economy – an economy that the West is pushing the Chinese to

---

[71] Cliford Krauss, "The lithium chase," *New York Times*, March 10, 2010.
[72] So we get this: Elisabeth Rosenthal, "Used batteries form U.S. expose Mexicans to risk," *New York Times*, December 9, 2011.
[73] *Eco-Economy*, p. 138 (my italics).

grow even faster to pull the rest of the world out of recession – and to feed its huge and growing population as more and more of its farmland is planted with factories.[74] It is scarcely necessary to point out that there are not enough soda cans on the planet to smelt down to support such exponentially increasing demand. So here again, *unless humanity places some non-market constraints on the consumption and use of these metals, then metals mining with all its associated destruction and pollution, will grow exponentially as well.* And much of this growing destruction will be directly attributable to the production of all the "green technology" that Hawken, Stern and others claim is going to save us.

II.C.6. Green manufacturing?

Much the same can be said for most manufacturing. Manufacturing and processing industries can't help but consume natural resources and produce pollution. The whole point of manufacturing is to turn raw materials into products. And there is hardly any manufacturing process that does not produce some waste and pollution as a by-product. In addition, many products themselves are also toxic and polluting and some, like pesticides, deliberately so. In *Natural Capitalism*, Hawken and the Lovins rhapsodized about the potential of miracle tech fixes, huge potential gains in efficiency, "dematerialization" of production. Lovins predicted (in 1999) that his designs for super-efficient "hybrid-electric hypercars" which could weigh two or three times less than a conventional car, use 92 percent less iron and steel, one-third less aluminum, three-fifths less rubber, and up to four-fifths less platinum and "last for decades" would soon be adopted by industry. Lovins even declined to patent his designs, offering his design ideas to the auto industry for free to encourage their adoption.[75] They called for transforming industry to "mimic nature" and recycle its own waste.[76] They lionized eco-capitalist heroes like John Browne, the CEO of British Petroleum who broke ranks with the oil industrial complex in 1997 declaring that man-made climate change was indeed a threat and announced that BP was no longer an oil company but an "energy company" that would transition into renewables like solar. They applauded when BMW promised to make its cars completely recyclable. They hailed The Body Shop, Patagonia, Herman Miller, 3M

---

[74] See e.g., the cover stories: David Leonhart, "Shop China Shop! Can the Chinese discover the urge to splurge?" *New York Times Magazine*, November 28, 2010; and "Buying up the World," *The Economist* for November 13-19, 2010.
[75] *Natural Capitalism*, chapter 2.
[76] Hawken, *Ecology of Commerce*, p. 38 (my italics). Brown, *Eco-Economy* chapters 4 and 12. Hawken and Lovins, *Natural Capitalism*, pp. 37-38 and passim.

Green capitalism: the god that failed

Company, Wal-Mart, even Dow Chemical and Dupont for their environmental initiatives. Above all, they celebrated Ray Anderson, founder and CEO of Interface, the world's largest modular carpet manufacturer, born-again environmentalist and hero of Joel Bakan's film *The Corporation* who credits reading Paul Hawken's *The Ecology of Commerce* with an epiphany that provoked him to remodel his company. In a message to his customers and employees in 1997, published in the *Interface Sustainability Report* of 1997 Anderson explained how he envisions "natural capitalism" in his own carpet factories:

> "As I write this, there is not an industrial company on earth that is sustainable in the sense of meeting its current needs without, in some measure, depriving future generations of the means of meeting their needs. When earth runs out of finite, exhaustible resources or ecosystems collapse, our descendants will be left holding the empty bag. But, maybe, just maybe, we can change this.

> "At Interface, we are on a quest to become the first sustainable corporation in the world... creating the technologies of the future – kinder, gentler technologies that emulate nature...

> "The technologies of the future will enable us to feed our factories with closed loop, recycled raw materials that come from harvesting the billions of square yards of carpets and textiles that have already been made – nylon face pile recycled into new nylon yard to be made into new nylon carpet; backing material recycled into new baking materials for new carpet; and in our textile business... polyester fabrics recycled into polyester fiber, then to be made into new fabrics – closing the loop; using those precious organic molecules over and over in cyclical fashion, rather than sending them to landfills... Linear must go; cyclical must replace it. That's nature's way. In nature there is no waste; one organism's waste is another's food. For our industrial process, so dependent on petro-chemical, man-made raw materials, this means technical "food" to be reincarnated by recycling into the product's next life cycle. Of course, the recycling operations will have to be driven by solar energy, too...

86

"We look forward to the day when our factories have no smokestacks and no effluents. If successful, we'll spend the rest of our days harvesting yesteryear's carpets, recycling old petro-chemicals into new materials, and converting sunlight into energy. There will be zero scrap going into landfills and zero emissions into the ecosystem. Literally, it is a company that will grow by cleaning up the world, not by polluting or degrading it."[77]

Ray Anderson is as sincere as he is eloquent and I will come back to discuss the results of his company's efforts below. But for all the eco-capitalist innovations of the 1980s and 90s, not much has changed in corporate board rooms. BP's Board fired John Browne in 2007, sold off his boutique solar power outfit, cashiered the *"Beyond Petroleum"* ads, and reassured investors that BP would not be deserting its core business in a misguided attempt to become an "energy" company, and that BP is emphatically an *OIL* company – as we've recently been reminded. Shell Oil, Chevron and other oil companies likewise sold off their solar power ventures and ramped up fossil-fuel exploitation, including tar sands and gas fracking.[78] Anita Roddick was forced out as CEO of the Body Shop after shareholders rebelled and demanded that management prioritize the bottom line over her political and environmental agenda. Ben and Jerry's sold out in 2000 to Unilever so no more 7½% for the planet. Patagonia still gives "1% for the planet" but why bother since, like Smith & Hawken, Patagonia is just another resource-hogging mail order company and almost all of its products are made of unsustainable synthetics. Herman Miller seems to have abandoned re-manufacturing customers' chairs, I would guess because, on second thought, there was more money to be made in the "linear" process of selling new ones and junking the old ones than in remanufacturing old ones. And from Detroit to Stuttgart to Tokyo, the world's auto makers have studiously ignored Amory Lovin's advice that "light and small is beautiful" in favor of the traditional industry wisdom which holds that "big car big profit, small car small profit". For all the hybrid hype, the auto show plug-ins, the Leafs and Volts, automakers still slight production of econoboxes and Priuses in favor of giant Toyota "Sequoias", Nissan Tundras, GM Sierras, Yukons and

---

[77] Quoted in *Natural Capitalism*, pp. 168-169. See also Ray C. Anderson, *Mid-Course Correction* (Atlanta: The Peregrinzilla Press, 1998), and Eileen P. Gunn, "The Green CEO," *Fortune*, May 24, 1999, pp. 190-200.
[78] Jad Mouawad, "Not so green after all: alternative fuel still a dalliance for oil giants," *New York Times* April 8, 2009.

Escalades, oversized and over-accessorized luxury Mercedes and BMWs – which remain everywhere the key to profitability.[79] Ten years after their introduction, hybrid cars accounted for just 2.5% of vehicle sales in the United States in 2008.[80] And even with the recent ramp-up, auto industry analyst J.D. Power and Associates predicts that global sales of hybrid electric and battery electric vehicles will reach just 5.2 million vehicles in 2020, or only 7.3 percent of the 70.9 million autos expected to be sold in that year.[81] And "hybrid" is an overstatement for most of these vehicles. Few electric hybrids are really fuel-efficient like the Toyota Prius. Most are just bloated luxury cars with a hybrid add-on that gets them a few miles per gallon better mileage than their non-hybrid equivalents – a little sales cachet but nowhere near enough to make any serious dent in global gasoline consumption, especially given that the global fleet of gasoline consuming cars on the road is growing by tens of millions every year. European automakers, *The Independent* reported, have "failed miserably" to meet their Kyoto pledges to tackle climate change by reducing emissions. Instead of focusing on boosting fuel economy, Landrover, Jaguar, Porche, BMW, Mercedes and even Volvo lobbied to win exceptions from EU-wide fuel economy standards in order to keep producing their profitable luxury gas guzzlers, some of which put out more than double the target

[79] Vanessa Fuhrmans, "Land yachts launch unexpected revival," *Wall Street Journal*, September 23, 2010. Nick Bunkley, "Sales of larger vehicles bring automakers an upbeat start for 2011," *New York Times*, February 2, 2011. Edward Niedermeyer, writing in the *New York Times* at the end of 2010 notes that for all the bailout promises by Obama that Detroit would "lead the world in building the next generation of clean cars," Detroit's sales of fuel efficient cars actually dropped in 2010. In fact, sales of *actual* cars has fell by about 6% even over 2009's anemic numbers while sales of light trucks, SUVs, minivans and crossovers were up by 16%: "Despite the rolling out of the much-hyped Cruze compact and the Volt plug-in hybrid, G.M. still sells half again as many trucks and SUVs as it does cars. This year, 73 percent of Chrysler's sales have been light trucks." He found the same trends with the imports. "The impressive per-unit profit margins" still gives automakers big incentives to push their luxury gas guzzlers over their gas sipping hybrids and econoboxes. See Edward Niedermeyer, "A green Detroit? No, a gulping one," *New York Times*, December 16, 2010. Also: Mike Spector and Joseph B. White, "Horsepower nation: new car models boast speed, size, power," *Wall Street Journal*, April 5, 2007; and idem, "Car-show dilemma: future isn't now," *Wall Street Journal*, April 5, 2007. And, to make matters worse: "Drivers offer a collective ho-hum as gasoline prices soar," *New York Times*, March 30, 2007.
[80] "2009 hybrid cars – year in review" post July 21, 2009 post at http://www.hybridcars.com/2009-hybrid-cars#market.
[81] J.D. Power and Associates, "Drive Green 2020: More Hope Than Reality," November, 2010, available at: http://businesscenter.jdpower.com/news/pressrelease.aspx?ID=2010213

fleet emissions level.[82] Finally, given the global glut of cars, the last thing the world's automakers want to do is make are cars that "last for decades". If anything, the auto makers Holy Grail would be to get their customers to junk their clunkers and buy a new one *every year*. The problem for eco-futurist inventors like the Lovins is that they understand technology but they don't understand capitalist economics.

II.C.7. Saint Ray Anderson and the limits of the possible

The seeming exception to the dismal trends reviewed above proves the rule: CEO Ray Anderson has probably pushed the limits of industrial environmentalism as far as it's humanly possible to go in an actual factory operating within the framework of capitalism. The late Ray Anderson was everybody's favorite eco-capitalist and he and his company Interface Inc. have been applauded by virtually every eco-futurist book written since the 1990s as *the* eco-capitalist example to emulate. But what Ray Anderson's case really shows us is the *limits of the possible*, especially under capitalism. For after almost two decades of sustained effort, the goal of "zero pollutants" is still as unreachable as ever at Interface Inc. It is not in the least to diminish Ray Anderson's sincerity, his passionate dedication, his efforts or his impressive achievements. But the fact is, according to *The Interface Sustainability Report* of 2009, Interface has "cut waste sent to landfills by more than half while continuing to increase production," "reduced greenhouse gas emissions by more than 30%," "reduced energy intensity by 45%," while "over 25% of raw materials used in interface carpet are recycled and biobased materials in 2007," and non-sustainable materials consumed per unit of product have declined from 10.2 lbs/yd^2 in 1996 to 8.6 lb/yd^2 in 2008.[83] *Read that last sentence again.* Make no mistake: these are impressive, even heroic industrial-environmental achievements. But if after more than a dozen years of sustained effort, the most environmentally dedicated large company in the United States, if not the entire world, can only manage to cut non-sustainable inputs from 10.2 to 8.6 pounds per square yard of finished product, to inject a mere *25%* recycled and biobased feedstock into its production process, so still requiring 75% of new, mostly petroleum-based non-sustainable feedstock in

---

[82] Cahal Milmo, "Car makers failing on emissions targets," *The Independent*, April 24, 2006. Vanessa Fuhrmans, "Porche presses for easier fuel rules," *Wall Street Journal*, March 26, 2010.
[83] These quotations and data are from the Interface Corporation website: http://www.interfaceglobal.com/Sustainability/Progress-to-Zero.aspx accessed Dec. 2009.

every unit of production, then the inescapable conclusion must be that *even the greenest businesses* are also on course to "destroy the world". So if the reality is that, when all is said and done there is only so much you can do in most industries, *then the only way to bend the economy in an ecological direction is to sharply limit production, especially of toxic products, which means completely redesigning production and consumption – all of which is impossible under capitalism.*

II.C.8. Taxing toxics and "natural capitalist" hypocrisy

Perhaps nowhere are the contradictions of the "tax the polluters" strategy more evident than with respect to the problem of taxing toxics. In his *Ecology of Commerce,* Paul Hawken says that *"Nothing* is more central to the argument of this book than the proposition that disposal of hazardous waste is *not* the root problem. Rather, it is the root symptom. The critical issue is the *creation* of toxic wastes." Hawken says we need a "restorative economy that thinks cradle-to-cradle, so that every product or by-product is imagined in its subsequent forms even before it is made... Rather than argue about where to put our wastes, who will pay for it, and how long it will be before the toxins leak into the groundwater, we should be trying to design systems that are elegantly imitative of climax ecosystems found in nature."[84] I couldn't agree more. But how can we ever get this under capitalism? For a start, who is the "we" Hawken is talking about? "We" ordinary citizens don't design manufacturing systems for the benefit of humankind, the natural world, and future generations of both. Corporations design manufacturing systems for the benefit of shareholders and their shareholders profit by manufacturing, spraying, pumping and dumping all those toxics all over the world and pushing the environmental costs of all this onto us – and that's the problem. "We" have no vote in the boardrooms and "we" do not tell the boards of directors what technologies to use or not use (nor does Hawken think "we" ought to either, see below). Corporate decisions are private decisions. Of course, we have a theoretically "representative" government which ought to express the will of the people if necessary, against the corporations. But as Hawken himself describes at some length, in our corporate dominated so-called democracy, government more often represents the interests of the corporations against the people than the people against the corporations.[85] So the problem for Hawken is that, since in his restorative economy, corporations would still rule production, CEOs and corporate boards would still make all the critical

---

[84] *Ibid.,* pp. 49, 54, and 71, my italics.
[85] *Ibid.,* pp. 108-119.

decisions, how then how can "we" the citizenry possibly redesign the system to serve the needs of humanity instead of to serve the needs of investors?

"Honor the market"

So what is Paul Hawken's solution to the nightmare of toxic chemical contamination? Ban or regulate their production? Compel industry to "redesign manufacturing systems so that they do not create hazardous and biologically useless waste in the first place." Not at all. For it turns out that, just like regular capitalists, "natural capitalist" Paul Hawken is more concerned to keep the government out of the market than he is to use government regulation to solve the problems caused by the market's "efficient" and "optimal" allocation of resources to poison people with toxic chemicals. Hawken says we should: *"Honor market principles.* No 'plan' to reverse environmental degradation can be enacted if it requires a wholesale change in the dynamics of the market."[86] So on this, Paul Hawken, Ronald Reagan and Milton Friedman would seem to agree: "Capitalism good. Government bad." Even if "business is destroying the world" as Hawken concedes, *still* he says:

> "...the guardian [his locution for 'the government'] of human and natural systems must *recognize its own limitations* in relation to commerce. *It cannot tell companies what to make and how. It does not have the ability to allocate resources in an efficient manner.*"[87]

So neither we the citizenry nor our nominal representative, the government, should tell polluters to stop producing all these hideously toxic chemicals and redesign their production. What then should the "guardian" do about the problem? Hawken says what the government should do is just *tax the polluters:*

> "[N]ot only should energy use be taxed more heavily, but so too, should all agricultural chemicals, from artificial fertilizers to toxic pesticides."[88]

So even in Hawken's "restorative economy", toxic polluters would still be free to spread their carcinogens everywhere – if they just *pay to pollute.* It is hard to

---

[86] *Ecological Commerce,* p. xv, italics in original.
[87] *Ibid.,* p. 168, my italics.
[88] *Ibid.,* p. 185.

imagine a more bankrupt strategy, guaranteed to fail, nor for that matter, a more hypocritical and *immoral* strategy. And the fact is, as Hawken knows very well, that this tax-the-polluters strategy is just a "toll road for polluters" and "a license to kill and maim".[89] If he read his own book, he would find this on page 66:

> "The problem with pollution permits is that they do just that – permit pollution. Illinois Power Company, which had been building a $350 million scrubber to remove sulfur dioxide at its plant, has decided to scrap the scrubber and buy pollution permits instead... By purchasing pollution credits, it can save $250 million over a 20-year period, and continue to buy high-sulfur coal from Illinois."[90]

Let's be clear about exactly what this means: it means that even in Hawken's utopian capitalist "restorative economy", those living downwind from this plant would continue to breathe in sulfur laden air *for decades*. And, not only sulfur. For burning coal also releases mercury, arsenic and other toxic pollutants. That means their kids will continue to suffer from increased birth defects, impaired intelligence, develop respiratory problems, asthma and cancer rates will continue to rise – and all this just so that investor-owners can maximize returns on the investments they have so "efficiently allocated" to this sector for more decades to come. So it turns out that in Hawken's eco-capitalist utopia, the role of "the guardian" is to protect business, not "we" the public. This is not quite what one would hope to hear from new-age thinking "restorative economy" eco-futurists like Paul Hawken.

And if this weren't enough, as part and parcel of their anti-government, anti-regulatory strategy, Paul Hawken, Lester Brown and Francis Cairncross also call for "tax shifting" – shifting from taxing income and capital (what they call "goods") to taxing "bads" like pollution.[91] *Quelle surprise.* Why is it always rich (and mostly white) guys who call for flat taxes? Aside from the fundamental unfairness of flat taxes, one wonders if it ever occurred to these brilliant theorists that if governments were actually to become dependent on pollution taxes for revenue, wouldn't they

---

[89] *Ibid.*, p. 83.
[90] *Ibid.*, p. 66.
[91] Hawken, *Ecology of Commerce*, pp.183-184 and passim. Brown, *Eco-Economy*, pp. 235-239. Cairncross, *op. cit.*, pp. 97-100.

then find it in their interest to let the pollution continue, if not actually increase, to augment revenues? What am I missing here?

III. Capitalism without consumerism?

Paul Hawken naturally looked to CEOs like himself who he imagined would be the prime agents of change "from above" as they revolutionized their mind-sets and redesigned production. Other eco-economic futurists have looked to bottom-up "consumer choice" as the driver forcing corporate producers to change. Still others, most recently Juliet Schor and Bill McKibben, duck the question of what to do about capitalism altogether, and argue that we should get out of the market to the extent we can, and retreat to the periphery in order to reduce consumerism and overconsumption. So the WorldWatch Institute, Juliet Schor, Bill McKibben and even Martha Stewart – all tell us to get off the treadmill of consumerism and "live simply".[92] They're right. We have to do that. Our very survival is at risk if we don't. Thus in its 2010 Report, subtitled "Transforming Cultures From Consumerism to Sustainability". The World Watch Institute tells us that:

> "Preventing the collapse of human civilization requires nothing
> less than a wholesale transformation of dominant cultural patterns.
> This transformation would reject consumerism... and establish in
> its place a new cultural framework centered on sustainability. In
> the process, a revamped understanding of "natural" would emerge:
> it would mean individual and societal choices that cause minimal
> ecological damage or, better yet, that restore Earth's ecological
> systems to health."[93]

But how can we "reject consumerism" when we live in a capitalist economy where, in the case of the United States, more than two-thirds of market sales, and therefore most jobs, depend on direct sales to consumers while most of the rest of the economy, including the infrastructure and military, is dedicated to propping up this consumerist "American way of life"? Indeed, most jobs in industrialized countries critically depend, not just on consumerism, but on ever-increasing *overconsumption.*

---

[92] Bill McKibben, *Eaarth* (New York: Henry Holt, 2010), Juliet Schor, *Plenitude* (New York: Penguin, 2010).
[93] *Op cit.*, pp. 3-4.

Green capitalism: the god that failed

We "need" this ever-increasing consumption and waste production because, without growth, capitalist economies collapse and unemployment soars, as we've seen. The problem with the Worldwatch Institute is that, on this issue, they're looking at the world upside down. They think that it is consumerist culture that drives corporations to overproduce. So their solution is to transform the culture, get people to read their Worldwatch reports and re-educate themselves so they understand the folly of consumerism and resolve to forego unnecessary consumption – *without transforming the economy itself*. But it's not the culture that drives the economy so much as, overwhelmingly, the economy that drives the culture. It's the insatiable demands of shareholders that drive corporate producers to maximize sales, therefore to constantly seek out new sales and sources in every corner of the planet, to endlessly invent, as the Lorax had it, new "thneeds" no one really needs, to obsoletize those thneeds just as soon as they've been sold, so the cycle can begin all over again. *This* is the driving engine of consumerism. Frank Lloyd Wright's apprentice Victor J. Papenek had it right:

> "Most things are not designed for the needs of people, but for the
> needs of manufacturers to sell to people."[94]

This means that *pace* the Worldwatch Institute, "consumerism" is not just a "cultural pattern," it's not just "commercial brainwashing" or an "infantile regression" as Benjamin Barber has it.[95] Insatiable consumerism is an everyday *requirement* of capitalist reproduction, and this drives capitalist invention and imperial expansion. No overconsumption, no growth, no jobs. And no "cultural transformation" is going to overcome this fundamental imperative so long as the economic system depends on overconsumption for its day-to-day survival.

IV. Climate change or system change?

The green capitalist project crucially rested on the assumption that the capitalists' goal of endless growth and profit maximizaton and society's goal of saving the

---

[94] Quoted in Giles Slade, *Made to Break* (Cambridge: Harvard, 2006), p. 52 (my italics). On this very interesting subject of the colossal waste of designed-in obsolescence and "forced consumption," Slade's book is excellent but Vance Packard's brilliantly ironic *The Wastemakers* remains unsurpassed (New York: David McKay, 1960).
[95] Bejamin R. Barber, *Consumed: How Markets Corrupt Children, Infantalize Adults, and Swallow Citizens Whole* (New York: Norton, 2007).

94

world from never-ending plunder and pollution could be "aligned" by imposing green taxes to discourage the generation of toxic waste, overconsumption of raw materials, the use of pesticides, the production of throwaway products, and could even, so Paul Hawken thought, "tax coal out of business". But this vision, as I have argued throughout this book, was always a delusion (albeit a profitable one for some) because, not only is it impossible to "align" these inherently contradictory interests, but to save the world, corporations would have to subordinate profit making to environmental goals: the coal industry, the makers of toxics pesticides, the generators of toxic wastes, the consumers of raw materials, the producers of throwaway products would all have to agree, in effect, to commit economic suicide. But how could they do this? How could they be responsible to society and their shareholders at the same time? The problem is always the private property form, especially the corporate form, and competitive production for market. Once capital is sunk into a given industry, staff and workers trained, markets secured – producers have every incentive and little choice but to grow their business or see their share prices fall as investors seek greener pastures. So Massey Coal has no choice but to mine and sell ever more coal until the ice caps melt – because that's the company's fiduciary and legal responsibility to its shareholders. Monsanto has no choice but to produce and sell as many ghastly pesticides as possible no matter the consequences for life on Earth. Formosa Plastics has no choice but to trash the world with plastic bags, and so on. Same with "green" businesses. Biofuels, wind power and organic crops – all might be environmentally rational here or there, but not necessarily in every case or forever. But once investments are sunk, green industries have no choice but to seek to maximize profits and grow forever regardless of social need and scientific rationality, just like any other for-profit business. So for example: Horizon Organic Dairy started out as a group of cooperatives paying premium prices to its small organic farmer suppliers. But once it was bought out by Dean Foods, the country's biggest milk distributor, and became a big publicly-traded corporation with its own centralized large-scale production operations, it dispensed with its founding pro-farmer ethic, cut payments to small suppliers, even used its scale of operations to undercut and drive them out of business while simultaneously adding to the nation's pollution by refrigerator-trucking its milk thousands of miles all over the country instead of buying it from local farmers. As one observer noted: "Dean's goal is to maximize shareholder value. That's not the same as maximizing farmer value." Nor is it the same as maximizing consumer value either, as Horizon is now ditching its organic commitment as well, adding synthetic additives to its milk.[96] And so it goes down the slippery slope. Sustainable production is certainly possible – but not under capitalism. To get a little ahead of the argument of this essay, I wouldn't think it's necessary to eliminate all markets in a sustainable ecological, even socialist, society. Offhand, I don't see the harm in small producers producing for market – family farmers, farmers markets, artisans, co-operatives, mom-and-pop restaurants, and so on. The problem is capitalist private property, especially in the corporate form: when owners become abstract anonymous "shareholders" concerned only to maximize profits, then all the evils of capitalism inevitably follow. To put it in Marxist terms, C-M-C (petty commodity production) seems harmless enough. The problem is M-C-M' – capitalism. I just don't see how large-scale production can be geared to the needs of society and the environment, and both for present and future generations, unless it is socialized and managed by democratic social institutions. But I'll take this up elsewhere.

One world, one people, one economy

We can't shop our way to sustainability because the problems we face cannot be solved by individual choices in the marketplace. In fact, most of the ecological problems we face from global warming to deforestation, from overfishing to pollution and species extinction – and many others, are way beyond the scope of companies, industries, even countries. They require concerted, large-scale national and international action. And they require direct economic planning at global, national and local levels. For example, the world's climate scientists tell us we're doomed unless we shut down the coal industry and sharply reduce our consumption of all fossil fuels. But even the world's largest corporations, such as Exxon Mobil, can't afford to take such losses, to sacrifice its owners – merely to save the humans.

Corporations can't make the socially and ecologically rational decisions that need to be made to save the humans because they represent only private particular interests, not the social and universal interests of humanity, the environment and future generations. But society *can* afford to close down coal, retrench oil production and

---

[96] Noel C. Paul, "Horizon Organic, now Dean Foods, threatens livelihood of organic farmers, *The Christian Science Monitor*, September 15, 2003 at: http://www.csmonitor.com/2003/0915/p16s01-wmcn.html. Cornucopia Institute: "New organic milk contains illegal synthetic additive," February 23, 2011 at: http://www.cornucopia.org/.

socialize those losses. Society *can* ration oil, like we did during World War II, and society *can* redeploy labor and resources to construct the things we do need to save the humans – like renewable energy, public transit, energy efficient housing for all and many other social needs that are currently unmet by the market system. In the final analysis, the only way to align production with society's interests and the needs of the environment is *to do so directly*. The huge global problems we face require the visible hand of direct economic planning to re-organize the world economy to meet the needs of humans and the environment, to enforce limits on consumption and pollution, to fairly ration and distribute the goods and services we produce for the benefit of each and every person on the planet, and to conserve resources so that future generations of humans and other life forms can also live their lives to the full. All this is inconceivable without the abolition of capitalist private property in the means of production and the institution of collective bottom-up democratic control over the economy and society. And it will be impossible to build functioning national and global economic democracies unless we also abolish global economic inequality. This is both the greatest moral imperative of our time and it is also essential to winning world-wide popular support for the profound changes we must make to prevent the collapse of civilization. A tall order to be sure. But we will need even taller waterproof boots if we don't make this happen. If Paul Hawken, Lester Brown, Francis Cairncross and Paul Krugman have a better plan, where is it?

Green capitalism: the god that failed

ESSAY 4 (2014)

Climate crisis, the deindustrialization imperative and the jobs vs. environment dilemma

Since the 1990s, climate scientists have been telling us that unless we suppress the rise of CO_2 emissions, we run the risk of crossing critical tipping points that could unleash runaway global warming, precipitate the collapse of civilization and perhaps even our own extinction. To suppress those growing emissions, climate scientists and the UN IPCC have called on industrialized nations to slash their CO_2 emissions by 80-90% below 1990 levels by 2050.[1] But instead of falling, CO_2 emissions have been soaring, even accelerating, breaking records year after year. In May 2013, CO_2 concentrations topped the 400ppm mark prompting climate scientists to warn that we're "running out of time", that we face a "climate emergency" and that unless we take "radical measures" to suppress emissions very soon, we're headed for a 4-degree or even 6-degree-Celsius rise before the end of the century. And it's not just climate scientists who are saying this, but also mainstream authorities including the World Bank, the IEA, and others. In 2012 the IEA warned that:

> "… no more than one-third of proven reserves of fossil fuels can be consumed prior to 2050 if we hope to prevent global warming from exceeding more than 2 degrees centigrade."[2]

In September 2014, the global accounting and consulting giant PricewaterhouseCoopers warned that:

> "For the sixth year running, the global economy has missed the decarbonisation target needed to limit global warming to 2°C... To avoid two degrees of warming, the global economy now needs to decarbonise at 6.2% a year, more than five times faster than the

---

[1] See e.g. James Hansen et al., "Target atmospheric CO_2: where should humanity aim?" *Open Atmospheric Science Journal* 2 (2008), p. 217, at
http://www.bentham.org/open/toasci/openaccess2.htm.
[2] IEA, *World Energy Outlook*, November 2012.

current rate, every year from now till 2100. On our current burn rate we blow our carbon budget by 2034, sixty six years ahead of schedule. This trajectory, based on IPCC data, takes us to four degrees of warming by the end of the century."[3]

Yet despite ever-more dire warnings from the most conservative scientific, economic and institutional authorities, despite record heat and drought, super storms and floods, melting ice caps, vanishing glaciers, "business as usual" prevails. Worse, every government on the planet is pulling out all the stops to maximize growth and consumption in the effort to hold on the fragile recovery.[4]

Extreme extraction, extreme consumption and the "Great Acceleration"

Around the world, governments are pushing "extreme extraction" – fracking, horizontal drilling, deep-ocean drilling and so on. In the U.S., President Obama congratulates himself for suppressing coal emissions and boosting auto mileage. But what do these trivial gains matter, really, when he's approved drilling under the Arctic Sea, re-opened the Eastern seaboard from Florida to Delaware (closed since the 1969 Santa Barbara oil spill), approved new and deeper drilling in the Gulf of Mexico even after the BP blowout, and brags that he's "added more oil pipeline than any president in history, enough to circle the earth and then some"?[5] In fact Obama has approved so much new oil and gas extraction that even Americans can't consume it all, so "Saudi America" has once again, after a forty-year hiatus, become an *oil exporter*. Canadians are doing their bit to cook the planet faster by extracting tar sands bitumen, the dirtiest of the dirtiest. China, Vietnam, the Philippines and Indonesia are scrambling to suck out the oil under the South China Sea. Even Ecuador is opening its previously off-limits Yasuni Biosphere Reserve to drilling by

[3] PWC, "Two degrees of separation: ambition and reality: low carbon index 2014," (September 2014), quote from the Foreword, at www.pwc.co.uk/assets/pdf/low-carbon-economy-index-2014.pdf.
[4] Ian Talley et al., "Global slowdown threatens recovery," *Wall Street Journal*, October 13, 2014. Landon Thomas Jr. and Liz Alderman, "IMF calls on cash-rich countries to step up large public investments," *New York Times*, October 5, 2014.
[5] Daniel Gilbert et al., "Oil boom returns to gulf after spill," *Wall Street Journal*, November 22-23,2014. "Obama says he's added pipeline 'to circle Earth and then some,'" *The Hill*, March 22, 2004 at http://thehill.com/policy/energy-environment/217607-obama-says-hes-added-enough-pipeline-to-encircle-earth-and-then-some-defends-position-on-keystone-pipeline.

Chinese oil companies. Around the world, we're consuming oil like there's no tomorrow. And not just oil, everything. Industrialized and industrializing nations are ravenously looting the planet's last resources – minerals, forests, fish, fresh water, everything, in what Michael KIare calls *The Race For What's Left*.[6]

Extreme extraction is driven by extreme production and consumption. Around the world, resource consumption is growing at several multiples the rate of population increase, driven by the capitalist engines of insidious commodification, incessant invention of new "needs", daily destruction of existing values by rendering more and more of what we've already bought disposable and replaceable, and, of course, by the insatiable appetites of the global 1%. Today, the global rich and the middle classes are devouring the planet in a kind of *après-moi-le-deluge* orgy of gluttony. Russian oligarchs party on yachts the size of naval cruisers. Mid-east oilogarchs build refrigerated cities in the middle of baking deserts. China's newly rich consume not just the usual baubles but also the world's last tigers, rhinoceroses, elephants, bears, pangolins and other rare exotic creatures, along with the last tropical forests – on an industrial scale.[7] Consumption by the global rich is beyond obscene but given its size, global middle-class consumption has vastly more impact on the planet's environment. For every Rolls Royce, there are thousands of Mercedes Benz. For every Learjet, hundreds of Boeing 777s.

Just look at China. Once China joined the capitalist world market, it has had to generate steady growth, at least 8% per year, just to keep up with its population which is still growing by around 7 million people per year, the equivalent of adding another Hong Kong every year. Further, given seething public anger and open, often violent protest against corrupt, crony capitalist Communist Party officials, the government has desperately sought to push growth and consumption to placate the opposition to coddle middle-class supporters. So it has built entire, completely unnecessary industries, including the world's largest automobile industry that China has no oil to fuel, which only adds layers to the country's gasping pollution, and which has brought transportation to a standstill in China's cities. In the 1980s, Beijing had a few thousand (rather vintage) cars and trucks and buses – but one

---

[6] New York: Picador 2012. See also, Ugo Bardi, *Extracted* (White River Junction: Chelsea Green 2013).
[7] Craig Simons, *The Devouring Dragon* (New York: St. Martins 2013). David Smith, "Elephant killings in Mozambique happening on 'industrialised' scale," *Guardian*, September 23, 2014. On China's ravenous consumption of global minerals, oil, natural gas, etc. see Elizabeth C. Economy and Michael Levi, By All Means Necessary (Oxford: OUP 2014).

could bicycle across the whole city in half an hour and you didn't have to wear a gas mask. Today, with 5 million cars on the city's streets, that journey can take hours by car, while on many days attempting that cross-town on your bicycle will put you in the hospital.[8] China is now consuming half the world's coal, more than half the world's steel, cement, copper and vast quantities of other resources to build unnecessary industries, unnecessary and dangerous dams, forests of useless vanity skyscrapers, to blanket the country with nearly empty high-speed rail networks and empty national expressways systems.[9] It has built millions of empty apartment blocks, even entire cities complete with shopping malls, universities, hospitals, museums – but no people. By one estimate, China's builders have put up more than 64 million surplus apartments, enough new flats to house more than half the American population, and they're adding millions more every year.[10]

Not so different here. In America, no one even talks about resource conservation anymore. That's so quaint, so seventies. So "small is beautiful" and all that. Since

---

[8] Li Jing and Nectar Gan, "Orange pollution alert raised as Beijing smog reaches 'hazardous' level," *South China Morning Post*, October 9, 2014. Idem, "Factories shut and buildings sites suspended as Beijing fights back against 'hazardous' smog," *South China Morning Post*, October 10, 2014. I discussed China's auto craze, and other missed opportunities, in my "Creative destruction: capitalist development and China's environment," *New Left Review* no. 222 (March/April 1997), pp. 1-41; and in "New problems for old: the institution of capitalist environmental irrationality in China," *Democracy & Nature*, Vol. 5, No.2 (1999) pp. 249-274.

[9] In June 2011, visiting NYU economist Nouriel Roubini told *Reuters*: "I was recently in Shanghai and I took their high-speed train to Hangzhou," he said, referring to the new Maglev line that has cut traveling time between the two cities to less than an hour from four hours previously. The brand new high-speed train is half-empty and the brand new station is three-quarters empty. Parallel to that train line, there is also a new highway that looked three-quarters empty. Next to the train station is also the new local airport of Shanghai and you can fly to Hangzhou," he said. There is no rationale for a country at that level of economic development to have not just duplication but triplication of those infrastructure projects." Kevin Lim, "'Meaningful probability' of a China hard landing: Roubini," *Reuters*, June 13, 2011.

[10] E.g. "Housing oversupply causing major crisis for Chinese economy, *NTD.TV*, May 16, 2014 at: http://www.ntd.tv/en/programs/news-politics/china-forbidden-news/20140516/143998-housing-oversupply-causing-major-crisis-for-chinese-economy-.html "China's real estate bubble," *CBS 60 Minutes*, August 11, 2013 at http://www.cbsnews.com/videos/chinas-real-estate-bubble/. Robin Banerji and Patrick Jackson, "China's ghost towns and phantom malls," *BBC News Online*, August 13, 2012 at http://www.bbc.com/news/magazine-19049254. Vincent Fernando, CFA, "There are now enough vacant properties in China to house over half of America," *Business Insider*, September 8, 2010 at http://www.businessinsider.com/there-are-now-enough-vacant-properties-in-china-to-house-over-half-of-america-2010-9.

the Reagan revolution it's been all about the "me" generation, about ever-more consumption, about "living very large" as the *Wall Street Journal* puts it. American houses today are more than twice the size on average, of houses built in the 1950s – even as families are shrinking. Most come with central air, flat-screen TVs in every room, walk-in closets the size of 1950s spare bedrooms. And those are just average houses. McMansions offer breathtaking extravagance and waste: swimming pools in the basement, next to the bowling alleys, next to the home theatre, next to the gym, the bar-lounge and game rooms. And those are just the basements. Upstairs there are the *Elle Décor* floors and furnishings of tropical hardwoods, *Architectural Digest* kitchens in marble and stainless steel, Waterworks© bathrooms, "bedroom suites" the size of small houses, lighting and audio "systems" and on and on.[11] Americans are said to use more electricity just for air conditioning than the entire continent of Africa uses for all purposes. Middle-class Americans don't even drive "cars" much anymore. They drive behemoth gas-hog SUVs and luxury trucks with names to match: giant Sequoias, mountainous Denalis and Sierras, vast Yukons, Tundras, Ticonderogas and Armadas. Many of these are more than twice the weight of American cars and pickup trucks in the 1950s. So much for Obama's plan to reduce U.S. global warming emissions by boosting fuel-economy.[12] Americans used to vacation at the nation's incomparable national parks and seashores. Now, increasingly, they jet off to far corners of the globe, or drift about the seas, on twenty-story high cruise ships bashing coral reefs.

Globalization and the advent of "The China Price" has also enabled industrialists to boost consumption by dramatically lowering the cost of light-industrial consumer goods production, so much so that they could finally annihilate most remaining "durable" goods categories – from refrigerators to shoes, and substitute cheaper, throwaway replacements.[13] Thus, "Fast Fashion" (aka "Trashion Fashion") from H&M, Target, Zara's and others, now rules the women's apparel market with clothes so cheap it's not worth the cost of dry-cleaning them. As Elizabeth Kline relates in her recent book *Overdressed: the Shockingly High Cost of Cheap Fashion*,[14] "seasonal shopping patterns have given way to continuous consumption".

---

[11] E.g., "Living very large," *Wall Street Journal*, February 10, 2012.
[12] Joseph White, "Fuel efficiency slows as SUV sales rise," *Wall Street Journal*, October 9, 2014.
[13] Alexandra Harney, *The China Price* (New York: Penguin 2008).
[14] New York: Penguin 2013.

Zara delivers new lines twice a week to its stores. H&M and Forever 21 stock new styles *every day*. In Kline's words:

> "Buying so much clothing and treating it as if it is disposable, is putting a huge added weight on the environment and is simply unsustainable."

To say the least. The U.S. cotton crop requires the application of 22 billion pounds of toxic weed killers, every year. Most fiber is dyed or bleached, treated in toxic chemical baths to make it brighter, softer, more fade resistant, water proof, or less prone to wrinkles. Upholstery fabrics and children's pajamas are treated with ghastly chemicals to make them stain resistant or fireproof. These toxic baths consume immense quantities of chemicals and water and it goes without saying that in China, the chemicals are routinely just dumped in rivers and lakes, untreated. Then after all the chemical treatments, the fabrics have to be dried under heat lamps. These processes consume enormous quantities of energy. The textile industry is one of the largest sources of GHG emissions in the world, and it's growing exponentially. In 1950, when there were around 2.5 billion people on Earth, they consumed around 10 million tons of fabric for all uses. Today, we are 7 billion, but we consume more than 70 million tons of fabric annually, nearly 3 times as much per person as we consumed in the 50s (hence those walk-in closets). Producing 70 million tons of fabric consumes astounding quantities of resources including more than 145 million tons of coal and between 1.5 and 2 trillion gallons of fresh water, every year. Synthetic fibers like polyester and such (now 60% of the market) are the worst. They consume between 10 and 25 times as much energy to produce as natural fibers.[15] In short, "fast fashion" is speeding the disposal of planet Earth. And that's just one disposables industry.

Shortly after the great People's Climate March in September, the World Wide Fund for Nature (WFF) issued its latest *Living Planet* Index detailing how human demands on the planet are extinguishing life on Earth. According to the report, the world has lost more than half of its vertebrate wildlife in just the last 40 years – 52% of birds, reptiles, amphibians, fish and mammals. Read that again: *HALF THE*

---

[15] Elizabeth Kline, op cit. pp. 3, 124-125. Energy consumption: FAO, cited in "Fabric and your carbon footprint, *O Ecotextiles*, March10, 2013, at
http://oecotextiles.wordpress.com/2013/10/03/fabric-and-your-carbon-footprint/.

WORLD'S VERTEBRATE WILDLIFE HAS BEEN LOST IN JUST THE LAST 40 YEARS.

> "The decline was seen everywhere – in rivers, on land and in the seas – and is mainly the result of increased habitat destruction, commercial fishing and hunting."

The fastest decline among animal populations were found in freshwater ecosystems, where numbers have plummeted by 75% since 1970. "Rivers are the bottom of the system" said Dave Tickner, WWF's chief freshwater adviser. "Whatever happens on land, it all ends up in the rivers." Besides pollution, human overconsumption for industrial purposes is massively straining the world's freshwater systems: "While population has risen fourfold in the last century, water use has gone up sevenfold."[16] All these trends are driving what scientists are calling "The Great Acceleration" of consumption that took off after WWII and has sharply picked up speed in the last three decades as China industrialized. Like some kind of final planetary "Going Out of Business" sale, we're consuming the world's last readily accessible natural resources in a generation or two – in a geological blink of an eye.

Capitalist priority to growth and profits over people and planet

What's more, given capitalism, we're all more or less locked into this lemming-like suicidal drive to hurl ourselves off the cliff. Whether as CEOs, investors, workers, or governments – *given capitalism*, we all "need" to maximize growth, therefore to consume more resources, and produce ever more pollution in the process – because companies need to satisfy the insatiable demands of investors and because *we all need the jobs.* That's why at every UN Climate Summit, the environment is invariably sacrificed to growth. As George Bush senior told the 1992 Climate Summit "The American way of life is not negotiable". Barack Obama is hardly so

---

[16] WWF, *The State of the Planet* at
http://www.wwf.org.uk/about_wwf/other_publications/living_planet_report_2014/#.VC_kNlb
rPRp.
The quotations are from Damian Carrington, "Earth has lost half of its wildlife in the past 40 years, says WWF," *Guardian*, September 29, 1014. See also George Monbiot's blog commentary: "It's time to shout stop on this war on the living world," *Guardian*, posted October 1, 2014 at
http://www.theguardian.com/environment/georgemonbiot/2014/oct/01/george-monbiot-war-on-the-living-world-wildlife.

crude and arrogant but his dogged refusal to accept binding limits on CO_2 emissions comes to the same thing. And Xi Jinping is certainly not going to sacrifice his "Chinese Dream" of great-power revival and mass consumerism on a hitherto unimagined scale, if Obama refuses to negotiate the planet-destroying "American way of life".

In short, *so long as we live under capitalism, today, tomorrow, next year and every year thereafter, economic growth will always be the overriding priority until we barrel right off the cliff to collapse.*

Where are the radical solutions?

Given the multiple existential threats to our very survival, you might expect that our leading environmental thinkers and activists would be looking into those "radical" solutions, and especially to be thinking "beyond capitalism".

Don't hold your breath.

From the perennial boosters of "green capitalism" and tech-fixits like Lester Brown, Al Gore and Jonathon Porrit, now reinforced by Paul Krugman,[17] to the apostles of "degrowth" and "steady state" capitalism like Herman Daly, Tim Jackson, the NEP's Andrew Simms, and Serge Latouche, for decades, mainstream debate has been frozen in a time warp of failed, bankrupt strategies, confined entirely within the framework of capitalism. Speaking for the mainstream, the UK's Jonathan Porrit, former Green Party Co-chair, Director of Friends of the Earth and so on, wrote in 2005 that:

> "Logically, whether we like it or not, sustainability is therefore going to have to be delivered within that all-encompassing capitalist framework. We don't have time to wait for any big-picture successor."[18]

Thus, even as his own studies demonstrate how (market-driven) out-of-control growth is burning up the planet, the world's preeminent climate scientist-turned-activist James Hansen can't bring himself to associate with the left, to think outside

---

[17] See his *New York Times* column of September 20, 2014.
[18] *Capitalism as if the World Matters* (London: Earthscan 2005) p. 84.

the capitalist box, to abandon his hopelessly contradictory and doomed-to-fail carbon tax scheme and join the struggle against the economic system that is destroying the future for his grandchildren.[19] And even as he cites ever-more dire warnings from climate scientists, Bill McKibben, the world's premier climate protest organizer, won't touch the third rail of capitalism because he isn't a socialist and because he doesn't want to alienate his liberal base and Rockefeller Foundation funders.[20]

"The problem isn't climate change, it's capitalism" – Naomi Klein

With her impassioned and eloquent blockbuster *This Changes Everything: Capitalism vs. the Climate*,[21] Naomi Klein seems finally to have broken open the mainstream discourse, cataloguing the failures, contradictions and corruptions of so-called green capitalism and raising anew the question of "big-picture successors". Klein nails climate change squarely on the door of capitalism with a withering indictment: "our economic system and our planetary system are now at war." Climate scientists tell us that:

> "...our only hope of keeping warming below... 2 degrees Celsius is for wealthy countries to cut their emissions by somewhere in the neighborhood of 8-10 percent a year."

> "The 'free' market simply cannot accomplish this task."

> *"What the climate needs to avoid collapse is a contraction in humanity's use of resources; what our economic model demands to avoid collapse is unfettered growth"* (p. 21, my italics).

In one of many vivid paragraphs in this powerful book she writes:

---

[19] On the contradictions of Hansen's "carbon tax and dividend" scheme, see my "Green capitalism: the god that failed," *Real-World Economics Review* no. 56 (2011) www.paecon.net/PAEReview/issue56/Smith56.pdf, reprinted in *truthout.org*. Cf. James Hansen, *Storms of My Grandchildren* (New York:Bloomsbury 2009)

[20] Vivian Krausse, "Rockefellers behind 'scruffy little outfit,'" *Financial Post*, February 14, 2013 at http://opinion.financialpost.com/2013/02/14/rockefellers-behind-scruffy-little-outfit/?__federated=1.

[21] New York (Simon & Schuster 2014)

Green capitalism: the god that failed

"Extractivism is a nonreciprocal, dominance-based relationship with the earth, one purely of taking. It is the opposite of stewardship, which involves taking but also taking care that regeneration and future life continue. Extractivism is the mentality of the mountaintop remover and the old-growth clear-cutter. It is the reduction of life into objects for the use of others, giving them no integrity or value of their own – turning living complex ecosystems into 'natural resources,' mountains into 'overburden' (as the mining industry terms the forests, rocks, and streams that get in the way of its bulldozers). It is also the reduction of human beings either into labor to be brutally extracted, pushed beyond limits, or, alternatively, into social burden, problems to be locked out at borders and locked away in prisons or on reservations. In an extractivist economy, the interconnections among various objectified components of life are ignored; the consequences of severing them are of no concern" (p. 169).

Klein presents a devastating critique of capitalism with consummate skill and dedication as a politically committed journalist. But when she turns to proposing solutions to the destructive and suicidal logic of capitalism, many – including myself – have found her maddeningly confusing, contradictory, even incoherent. She neither puts forward an alternative to capitalism nor a plausible way to stop global warming within the framework of capitalism. The urgency of the climate crisis, Klein says, "tells us all to revolt". But revolt for what since she rules out socialism *a priori*? She "shuns the never-never land of capitalism's global overthrow" as Rob Nixon put it in his *New York Times* review while the reviewer for the right-wing *Telegraph* told its readers to relax, Klein is "no advocate of socialism". She rails against the outrages of capitalism. But since she stops short of calling for "system change" to, say, eco-socialism, it's hard to see how we can make the profound, radical changes she says we need to make to prevent ecological collapse. Klein calls for "managed degrowth" of the "careless" economy of fossil-fuel "extractivism" – offset by the growth of a "caring economy" of more investment in emissions reduction, environmental remediation, the caregiving professions, green jobs, renewable energy, mass transit and so on (pp. 88-95). I couldn't agree more. But how can we change these priorities when the economy remains in the hands of huge corporations who want to keep the priorities just as they are?

Here and there argues for economic planning and democratic control of the economy. So she says we need a:

> "...comprehensive vision for what should emerge in place of our failing system, as well as serious strategies for how to achieve those goals" (p. 9-10).

> "...we need an entirely new economic model and a new way of sharing this planet" (p. 25).

She says the:

> "...central battle of our time [is] whether we need to plan and manage our societies to reflect our goals and values, or whether that task can be left to the magic of the market" (p. 40), and:

> "....a core battle must be the right of citizens to democratically decide what kind of economy they need" (p. 125).

But since she does not explicitly call for abolishing capitalism, for socializing the economy and instituting society-wide, bottom-up, democratic economic planning, how is society supposed to democratically decide what kind of economy they want?

Under capitalism, those decisions are the prerogative of corporate boards. We don't get to vote on the economy, but we need to. She calls for "slapping the invisible hand" of the market and "reining in corporate greed" (pp. 120, 125). But she does not call for nationalizing or socializing the major corporations, for abolishing private property in the major means of production (the institutional basis of corporate greed) and replacing it with public ownership of the major means of production. She rejects "the reigning ideology" the "economic model" of "market fundamentalism" and "neo-liberalism" (pp. 19-21). But rejecting market fundamentalism and neo-liberalism is not the same thing as rejecting capitalism. "Slapping the invisible hand" of the market system is not the same thing as replacing the invisible hand of the market with the visible hand of generalized economic planning. She rejects the "free" "unfettered" market (p. 21) but she does not reject the market system *per se*.

So, for example, she supports feed-in tariffs "to ensure that anyone who wants to get into renewable power generation can do so in a way that is simple, stable, and profitable" (p. 131). She does call for reviving FDR-style industrial planning to prioritize public transit and smart grids, generate "green" jobs and such (pp. 127, 133). She calls for returning some utilities to the public sector, for decentralizing and localizing control over utilities, energy and agriculture (pp. 21, 120, 130-134, and chapter 4 passim), and for taxing the rich to pay for more public spending. But all fits comfortably within the framework of a standard Keynesian capitalist economy. She doesn't call for generalized economic planning or public ownership of the means of production.

In her vision of the future, private property will still rule, corporations will still run the world's economies and capitalist governments will still run politics. Thus:

> "Since the [oil] companies are going to continue being rich for the foreseeable future, the best hope of breaking the political deadlock is to radically restrict their ability to spend their profits on buying, and bullying, politicians ...

> "...the solutions are clear. Politicians must be prohibited from receiving donations from the industries they regulate, or from accepting jobs in lieu of bribes, political donations need to be both fully disclosed and tightly capped..." (pp. 151-152).

How is this situation going to change?

Klein's strategy for social, political and economic change boils down to protest and "blockadia":

> "Only mass social movements can save us... If enough of us decide that climate change is a crisis worthy of Marshall Plan levels of response, then it will become one, and the political class will have to respond, both by making resources available and by bending the free market rules that have proven so pliable when elite interests are in peril" (pp. 6, 152, 450).

But the question is, why would any of this change? How are "elite interests in peril" when the basic system of capitalist power and property remain in force? And how could corporations "bend the rules of the market" enough to save the humans, even if they were so inclined, and still stay in business in a competitive market economy against, say, the Chinese? What's more, the prospects for building protests against this system are sharply limited if there's no alternative out there. Three hundred thousand people came out in the streets of New York in September 2014 to protest that the powers that be do *something* to stop climate change. But they were not calling for "degrowth" or industrial shutdowns. Given capitalism, how could they? Unless we can come up with an alternative economic system that will guarantee reemployment for all those millions of workers in industries around the world that will have to be retrenched or shut down to get that 90% reduction CO_2 emissions, we won't be able to mobilize them to fight for the radical changes they and we all need to save ourselves. If Naomi Klein really means to call for a mass movement to degrow the economy within the framework of capitalism, that sounds like a non-starter to me.

Given her confusion and lack of clarity, the message of her book reads like Occupy. When New York bankers replied to the Occupy movement in 2011: "Don't like capitalism? What's your alternative?" For all its audacity and militancy, Occupy had no alternative to offer. Klein herself says:

> "...saying no is not enough. If opposition movements are to do more than burn bright and then burn out, they will need a comprehensive vision for what should emerge in the place of our failing system, as well as serious political strategies for how to achieve those goals" (pp. 9-10).

Yet Klein doesn't present any comprehensive vision for what should replace our failing system, capitalism, either.

The necessity of economic planning and public ownership of the major means of production

The only way we can brake fossil fuel-driven global warming is to socialize the fossil fuel industries, buy them out if necessary, but nationalize them, socialize them one way or another, so we can phase them out, conserve the fuels we absolutely can't do without, at least for a transition period, and reallocate their resources to things society does need. And not just the fossil fuel industries and electric utilities.

We would have to socialize most of the rest of the industrial economy as well, because if we suppress fossil fuel production by anywhere near 90%, then autos, petrochemicals, aviation, shipping, construction, manufacturing and many other industries would grind to a halt. Naomi Klein quotes a top UN climate expert who remarked, not entirely tongue-in-cheek, that given all the failed promises to date, given the backsliding and soaring CO_2 emissions, "the only way" climate negotiators "can achieve a 2-degree goal is to shut down the whole global economy."[22] Well, I don't know if we need to shut down the whole world industrial economy, but it's difficult to see how we can halt the rise in GHG emissions unless we shut down a whole lot of industries around the world.

The imperative of deindustrialization in the North

The "degrowth" people are right in part. But there are two huge problems with their model. First, any degrowth serious enough to sharply reduce CO_2 emissions would bring economic collapse, depression and mass unemployment before it brought sustainability. That's why *décroissance* fantasists like Serge Latouce call for degrowth but then, *quelle surprise,* don't want to actually degrow the GDP, let alone overthrow capitalism.[23] But there is just no way around this dilemma. With no way to magically "dematerialize" production so we can keep growing the economy without growing emissions, then cutting CO_2 emissions by even 50% let alone 90% would require retrenching and closing *large numbers of large and small corporations around the world* and that means *gutting the global GDP –* with all that implies. With most of the capitalist world economy on the verge of falling back into recession, even the *slightest hint* of any slowdown in plundering the planet sends markets tumbling. Even the thought that *Ebola* could slow the growth of trade sent jitters through the markets.[24] That's why, given capitalism, no one except (securely tenured) professors would ever take the idea of "degrowth" seriously.[25] And yet, given that we live on a finite planet, the fact remains that we can't save humanity unless we radically degrow the overconsuming economies in the North. So we do need degrowth. But the only way to get "managed degrowth" without ending up in another Great Depression, is to do so in an entirely different, non-market or

---

[22] Klein, *op. cit.* p. 87.

[23] Serge Latouche, *Farewell to Growth* (Malden MA: Polity Press 2009), pp. 66, 91 and passim.

[24] E.g., "Global growth fears send markets tumbling," *BBC News*, October 7, 2014.
"Dow tumbles as Ebola fears, in part, rattle markets," *NBC News,* October 15, 2014.

[25] "Beyond growth or beyond capitalism," *op cit.*

mostly non-market economy.

The second problem is that we don't need to "degrow" the whole economy. We need to completely abolish all kinds of useless, wasteful, polluting, harmful industries. Yet we also need to grow *other parts* of the economy: renewable energy, public health care, public transit, the bicycle industrial complex, durable and energy efficient housing, durable vehicles, appliances and electronics, public schools, public services of all kinds, environmental remediation, reforestation – the "caring economy" Naomi Klein talks about and which I have also written about. But the problem for Jackson, Klein and the rest of the degrowth school, is that given private property in the means of production, given the anarchy of production for market, given the "iron law" of priority to profit maximization, and given the imperatives of competition – there is just no way to prioritize people and planet over growth and profits in a market economy.

The only way to rationally reorganize the economy, to de-emphasize the "careless" industries and emphasize the "caring" industries, is to do this ourselves, directly, by consciously and collectively and democratically planning most of the industrial economy, even closely coordinating most of the world's industrial economies. To do this we would have to socialize virtually all large-scale industry (though, as I've said elsewhere, this does not mean we need to nationalize "mom & pop" restaurants, small-scale owner-operator businesses, worker cooperatives, small farmers, and the like, though even some of those would need to be tightly regulated). Naomi Klein is rightly skeptical about "energy nationalization on existing models", because Brazil's Petrobras or Norway's Statoil are "just as voracious in pursuing high-risk pools of carbon as their private sector counterparts."[26] But that's because the "existing model" they operate in is the capitalist world economy – so even if they're state-owned, they still need to abide by the rules of the market. This only underlines the eco-socialist argument that the only way we can stop global warming and solve our many interrelated environmental crises is with a mostly-planned, mostly publicly-owned, mostly non-market economy.[27]

---

[26] Klein, *op. cit.* p. 130.
[27] See my "Capitalism and the destruction of life on earth: six theses on saving the humans," *Real-World Economics Review* no. 64 (2013)

Green capitalism: the god that failed

Contraction and convergence

Given the state of the planet right now, the only way we can move toward sustainability is if the industrialized nations and China impose an *emergency contraction*: radically suppress, and in many cases close down all kinds of useless, superfluous, wasteful, polluting industries and sectors. At the same time, most of the global South is far from overconsuming the planet; they're underconsuming almost everything. Four hundred million Indians lack electrical service. Most of the developing world still lacks basic infrastructure, schools, healthcare, decent housing, jobs and much else. So the South certainly needs "development" but if the South develops on the basis of capitalism, like China, this will only wreck the world faster. Global sustainability thus requires *selective de-industrialization in the North combined with sustainable industrialization in the South* – a global contraction and convergence centered on a sustainable (and hopefully happy) medium that will put the brakes on GHG emissions and enable the whole world to live in tolerable comfort while conserving resources for our children and set aside sufficient resources for the other species with whom we share this planet to live out their lives.

Environmentalists often argue that if we just switch from fossil fuels to renewables like solar and wind, then we'll be on the road to sustainability. Renewable energy is certainly part of the solution, but it is by no means most of it. That's because GHG emissions are produced *across the entire economy*, not only or even mainly by electric generating stations. As the table below shows, globally, electricity generation accounts for only around 17% of GHG emissions (25% including heat), industry about 15%, transportation 14%, agriculture, especially carbon-intensive agribusiness 14%, deforestation another 12%. These are global averages and individual country emissions vary widely. In the U.S., electricity generation (including heat) accounts for 32% of GHG emissions, transportation close behind at 28%, industry 20%, agriculture 10% (2011).[28] In China, electricity and heat account for 50% of CO_2 emissions, industry 31%, transportation 8% (2011).[29] In France electricity accounts for a trivial share of the country's CO_2 emissions because nearly 80% of France's electricity is produced by nuclear power plants.

---

[28] U.S. EPA, "Sources of greenhouse gas emissions 2012" at
http://www.epa.gov/climatechange/ghgemissions/sources/electricity.html.
http://cait.wri.org/cait.php?page=sectors.
[29] IEA, "CO_2 Emissions from fuel combustion 2013," (OECD/IEA 2013), pp. 26-27 at
http://www.iea.org/publications/freepublications/publication/co2emissionsfromfuelcombustio
nhighlights2013.pdf.

Climate crisis, deindustrialization and jobs vs. environment

World GHG Emissions in 2005 by Sector

Energy	
Electricity and heat	24.9%
Of which:	
Electricity:	17%
Heating:	5%
Other energy:	less than 3%
Industry	14.7%
Transportation	14.3%
Other fuel consumption	8.6%
Fugitive emissions	4.0%
Agriculture	13.8%
Deforestation and other land use changes 12.2%	
Industrial processes	4.3%
Waste	3.2%

Source: World Resources Institute (WRI) World Greenhouse Gas Emissions: 2005 (Washington DC: WRI, 2009) at http://www.wri.org/chart/world-greenhouse-gas-emissions-2005.

Thus, the first thing to be noted from this table is that *even if we shut down every coal, oil and gas-fired electric generating plant in the world tomorrow and replaced them all with solar and wind, that would reduce global CO_2 emissions by only around 17% (25% including heat).* That means that if we want to cut CO_2 emissions by 90% in the next 35 years we would have to drastically suppress emissions across the rest of the economy. We would have to drastically retrench and even close down – not only fossil fuel companies like Peabody Coal and ExxonMobil – but also the industries that are based on fossil fuels: autos, aircraft, airlines, shipping, petrochemicals, manufacturing, construction, agribusiness, refrigeration and air conditioning companies like GM, Boeing, United Airlines, FedEx, Cargill, Carrier, and so on.

Green capitalism: the god that failed

If we're going to stop the plunder of the planet's last accessible resources, then we would also have to retrench or close down lots of mines, lumber companies, pulp and paper and wood products companies, industrial fishing operations, industrial farming, CAFO livestock operations, junk food producers, private water companies, disposable products of all sorts, packaging, retail, and so on, companies like Rio Tinto, Georgia Pacific, Coca Cola, MacDonalds, Tyson Foods, H&M, Walmart, etc.

And if we're going to stop fouling our nest, poisoning our fresh water, soil, the oceans and atmosphere with myriad toxic chemicals, then we would have to shut down, or at the very least, drastically retrench and rigorously regulate the world's worst toxic producers – chemicals, pesticides, plastics, etc., companies like Monsanto, Dow, and Dupont, and others.

I know this sounds completely crazy. But I don't see what other conclusion we can draw from the scientific evidence. If we have to decarbonize by 6-10% per year, to 90% below 1990 levels by 2050 to contain global warming, how can we do that without radically retrenching and closing down large numbers of power plants, mines, factories, mills, processing and other industries and services from the U.S. to China? An unpleasant thought. But what other choice do we have? If we don't radically suppress GHG emissions we're headed for global ecological collapse. And if we don't stop looting the world's resources and poisoning the air, land and water with every manner of toxics, what kind of world are we going to leave to our children?

Besides, these industries and companies are hardly immortal. Most of the worst environmentally destructive industries in the U.S. businesses have been built or massively expanded since WWII. Most of China's resource-wasting and polluting industries have all been built in the last 20-30 years. Why can't these be dismantled or repurposed, if we need to do so to save the humans? This will cause dislocation for sure. But that's nothing compared to the dislocation we will face when droughts bring on the collapse of agriculture in the United States, when Shangahi and the Shenzhen sink beneath the waves, if we don't suppress CO_2 emissions, now.

In the last analysis, the only way to save the planet is to stop converting so much of it into "product." Leave the coal in the hole, the oil in the soil, the gas under the grass – but also leave the trees in the forests, the fish in the sea, the minerals in the mountains, and find ways for our billions to live lightly on the Earth.

Climate crisis, deindustrialization and jobs vs. environment

I'm no Luddite (though as a skilled craftsman, I'm a sympathizer). I'm not suggesting we abandon modernity and go back to living in some pre-industrial state. After all, Europeans currently generate barely half the GHG emissions as Americans and they're not living in caves. Actually, they live a lot better than Americans, though they consume less, in large part because they don't fetishize individualism, they provide much more for each other through collective social services, publicly-funded health care, and so on – so they don't need to earn as much to live better than Americans. Even so, West European consumption is still far from sustainable. Europeans still need to suppress CO_2 emissions, curb many other pollutants, and end useless consumption as well. What difference does it make, for example, if the Germans get 30% or even 100% of their electricity from renewable sources, if what they use that electricity for is to power huge factories producing an endless waste stream of oversize, over-accessorized, designed-to-be-obsolesced Mercedez Benz global warmers? What kind of "sustainability" is that?

I'm for modern technology – up to point. I imagine any modern ecological society will still have some cars, planes, chemicals, plastic, cell phones and so on, though many fewer. The problem is that so much of what we produce today is so unnecessary, harmful and unsustainable. Even though an ecological society would still need some cars and trucks, for example, to supplement expanded public transportation, it would not need hundreds of millions of new models every year. That's just such a waste. Cars could easily be built like my old '62 VW Beetle. That car can last practically forever since it was simple, built to be easily rebuilt, and every part is still in production. Why can't we make the few cars and trucks we need to be equally rebuildable, upgradeable, so they can last for decades, if not practically indefinitely, instead of the 7 to 10 years they typically last these days? And why can't we share them, in public car-sharing collectives, instead of having millions of privately-owned cars parked on the streets most of the time? The same with many other industries. China's Ministry of Housing admits that many of the "tofu" and "fast food" apartment blocks builders have thrown up in the building boom of recent years are so shabby "they can only last 20 or 30 years."[30] Disposable housing? Why can't we build housing to last centuries, like the gorgeous cities of Europe, or like China's own cities used to be built before the current government demolished Ming and Ch'ing era neighborhoods to build tofu apartment blocks and useless vanity skyscrapers? This would save mountains of stone, steel, aluminum, glass, Malaysian

---

[30] Quoted in Lu Chen, "China's apartments built 'fast food' style starting to crumble," *Epoch Times*, April 10, 2014.

forests of wood flooring. China could close most of its coal-fired power plants, clear the air and replace them with *nothing* if they simply gave up manufacturing the export junk we don't need and stopped building disposable housing and useless skyscrapers, roads and cars they don't need either. Or again, Apple's brilliant engineers could easily design iPhones to last decades, to be upgradeable and completely recyclable. If we need smart phones in an ecological society, fine, but they need to be built like those Beetles. This would save lakes of petrochemicals, heavy metals, rare earths, not to mention the lives of Foxconn workers who jump out of their dormitory windows to their deaths in despair over the insane pace of production, the boredom of 8-16 hour days of repetitive work, and the hopelessness of their assembly-line future. Of course, Apple would go out of business tomorrow if couldn't sell millions of "new" iThings every year. But the endless production of disposable phones, clothes, houses, appliances, cars and more is killing the planet. So which is it to be? We save Apple or we save the humans (and the whales)?

Jobs vs. environment is no myth

The difficulty of course, aside from the other huge difficulty of how to sack capitalism, is that if we have to deindustrialize to save the environment then this is going to cost jobs, not just a few coal-mining jobs but millions of jobs across the industrialized and industrializing world from the U.S. to Europe, South Africa, Australia and China. Environmentalists often casually assert that "jobs vs. environment is a myth." I beg to differ. This is by far the biggest dilemma the environmental movement faces – and there are no simple "green jobs" "win-win" solutions – at least not within the framework of capitalism. In China's Guangdong Province alone there are something like 40 million manufacturing workers (that is, by comparison, more the three times the size of the entire U.S. manufacturing workforce), the bulk of them dedicated to producing unsustainable, designed-to-be-obsolesced, disposable products from plastic toys, shoes, clothes, flimsy appliances, short-lived tools, Christmas junk, to the highest tech iPhones, laptops, Panasonic flat-screen TVs, automobiles, and more. As China opened up to become the workshop of the world, with its bottomless supply of ultra-cheap labor, many of the world's dirtiest, most wasteful, and least sustainable industries migrated to its coastal enclave export zones. This production is poisoning Guangdong's rivers, aquifers, farm fields, food supplies and the air people breathe. A recent survey found that 40% of the rice served in Guangzhou restaurants was tainted with cadmium, a highly toxic heavy metal with serious health implications. Why? Because industrial plants including battery makers for those electronic devices and vehicles, the source of the cadmium, have been built right next to rice paddies. This is everywhere in China. Public water supplies throughout the region and most of China are, by government standards, "severely polluted" with industrial chemicals, heavy metals and myriad other toxics. A recent government survey found that 64% of urban drinking water supplies were unfit for human consumption.[31] Croplands are heavily polluted with pesticides, heavy metals, arsenic, and other toxics. Already 20% of farmland has been declared too toxic to farm and that is widely thought to be an underestimate. The food is so polluted the middle classes try to import as much as they can from the West, clearing out shelves of baby formula from New Zealand to Holland. Then there's the air pollution. Most of this pollution comes from the factories where those tens of millions of workers are laboring day and night producing all these unnecessary, short-lived, throwaway, disposable products, mostly for export. What kind of "miracle" is this?

I just don't see how China can put the brakes on its own ecological self-destruction, the destruction of the health of its people and rein in the country's surging CO_2 emissions without closing down most of those industries. That is a problem. Forty million unemployed workers is a big problem. And that's just Guangdong.[32] But undrinkable water, unsafe food, unbreathable air, polluted farmland, the epidemic of cancer, rising temperatures and rising seas along coastal China are bigger problems. So there's just no way around this very inconvenient truth. Making bad stuff has to stop; stopping it will unemploy vast numbers of workers, and other, non-destructive jobs have to be found for them. We're riding a global engine of ravenous resource consumption. We all know this can't go on forever but the thought that it might come to a stop is so terrifying to all of us that most of the time we just want to live in denial. No wonder even many eco-socialists resist accepting the need to "degrow" the economy because, under capitalism, that would mean not just austerity but starvation. That's a hard sell.

---

[31] Cecilia Torajada and Asit K. Biswas, "The problem of water management," *China Daily*, March 5, 2013. Gong Jing and Liu Hongqiao, "Half of China's urban drinking water fails to meet standards," *China Dialogue*, June 6, 2013 at https://www.chinadialogue.net/article/show/single/en/6074-Half-of-China-s-urban-drinking-water-fails-to-meet-standards.
[32] China has more than 104 million manufacturing workers – about twice the number of manufacturing workers in the United States, Canada, Japan, France, Germany, Italy and the UK *combined*. Harney, *op. cit.* p. 8.

Green capitalism: the god that failed

From Pennsylvania to Colorado, the surge in oil and gas production has brought the first good-paying jobs many workers in those states have seen in decades and revived steel mills, abandoned industries and downtrodden towns across the industrial heartland – thanks to fracking.[33] In Canada, tar sands mining companies and pipeline companies have posted paying jobs to impoverished native Canadians. Indigenous resistance has powered the fightback against extreme extraction, tars sands, pipelines and polluted landscapes from Nigeria to Equador, Canada to the U.S., because these practices destroy their lands, waters and communities, and doom their children's futures. But indigenous communities are often split because they're so poor and so desperately need the jobs. Naomi Klein notes that, while many courageously and selflessly resist these extractive industries, "many indigenous people would view the extractive industries as their best of a series of bad options..." in communities with no other economic development, no other jobs or training. "As the offers from industry become richer ... those who are trying to hold the line too often feel they have nothing to offer their people but continued impoverishment." A long-time Northern Cheyenne opponent of coal development told her that, "I can't keep asking my people to suffer with me."[34]

This is the tragedy of capitalism versus the environment. What we need to do to save the humans tomorrow means economic collapse and mass unemployment today. Given that threat, unless workers are offered other jobs at comparable pay, not just "retraining" and a few months of unemployment insurance, then it will be difficult if not impossible to win many of them, and their unions, to support the sorts of radical changes we need to make to save them, us, and the planet. That's why we have to fight for a full-employment economy, and that means an eco-socialist economy.

Green jobs are fine, as far as they go. But I don't see many millions of jobs polishing solar panels. And when I've visited windmill farms there's no one around. We certainly can't save the world by producing millions of electric cars instead of millions of gasoline cars because they're both polluting and both consume too many resources. Given a finite planet, we don't need to produce green cars so much as massively *fewer* cars, fewer airplanes, fewer ships, fewer buildings, fewer iPhones, much less electricity in the North (though much more in the South) fewer processed foods, and lots of other things we currently take for granted. We need to do a whole

---

[33] Nelson Schwartz, "Boom in energy spurs industry in rust belt," *New York Times*, September 8, 2014.
[34] *This Changes Everything*, p. 86.

lot less manufacturing, less mining, less drilling, less production, less "value added" processing, especially in the North. In Naomi Klein's words: "Humanity has to go a whole lot easier on the living systems that sustain us, acting regeneratively rather than extractively." That means we need to create a completely different kind of economy, an in which "work" does not necessarily mean turning natural "resources" into product so much as living, as Klein says, "reciprocally" with nature.

Ecosocialism, "sacrifice" and slow food

Contraction and convergence, and eco-socialism based on planning, democracy, equality and sharing are, I think, the only path to a sustainable economy and society. Corporations can't afford to put themselves out of business but society can afford to socialize those costs. It has to. And only society can reorganize production to provide those alternative jobs. There's plenty of work to be done. It's just work that's never profitable to capitalists. Instead of building a disposable world, we need to build a durable world. Instead of producing junk we don't need, we need to produce the things we're not producing now, especially those "caring industries". We need to construct universal public health care, universal high-quality public education, universal organic farming, environmental remediation, retrofitting, upgrading and restoring existing housing, building eco-housing, co-housing, reforestation, more cultural and recreational opportunities. Instead of consuming the planet as fast as possible, *we need an entirely different mode of life based on minimizing, not maximizing resource consumption, on living lightly on the planet, on conserving resources for future generations an sharing them with each other and with other species.*[35]

Does this mean that we have to "sacrifice," accept a lower standard of living? Well, if by "standard of living" we mean American-style instant gratification and insatiable consumerism, then yes. Goodbye to all that. Limitless free choice is great. But there are costs to that, unbearable costs if we want to preserve a world worth living in. I'm sure we'll have to give up new cars, new iPhones every year, jet flights whenever we like, ever-wider screen TVs. Do we really need those to be happy? We'll have to make do with bicycles and public transit for most getting around. But it turns out people are healthier and happier when walk, bike, and don't

---

[35] Adam Parsons, "Sharing as the new common sense in a post-growth world," *Share the World's Resources*, August 29, 2014 at http://www.sharing.org. The website has a number of other excellent articles on this and related topics.

have to drive.[36] We'll have to give up Fedex overnight book deliveries from Amazon. But wouldn't the revival of local bookshops be worth the "sacrifice"? We'll have to give up fossil-fuel powered leaf-blowers and riding lawnmowers. I'll vote for that. We'll have to radically reduce international trade and re-produce most of what we need, and used to produce, locally, instead of by semi-slave labor in China. We'll have to get used to seasonal crops again, to give up fresh raspberries air-freighted to my local New York supermarket in the middle of winter from Chile because that's just ridiculously unsustainable. On the other hand, seasonal crops – asparagus in March, strawberries in May and June, apples and peaches all summer long, blackberries in September, squash in October, were one of the great joys of my childhood growing up in Washington. I could suffer those again. Actually, I expect we'll have to give up meat and become vegetarians or mostly vegetarians because the environmental cost of feeding billions of people a meat-based diet is just wildly unsustainable.[37] It's not so nice for the critters we eat either. But we'll be healthier for it. We'll have to make do with "slow food", "slow fashion" and "slow travel" But what's the rush? As Carl Honoré, a founder of the Slow Movement put it, the Slow philosophy:

> "… is not about doing everything at a snail's pace. It's about seeking to do everything at the right speed. Savoring the hours and minutes rather than just counting them. Doing everything as well as possible, instead of as fast as possible. It's about quality over quantity in everything from work to food to parenting."[38]

The trade-offs are more than worth it. As a professional carpenter-builder, I can't wait to "sacrifice" by turning my attention to building, re-building, upgrading and restoring homes for people who need them, public buildings for the common good, restoring our cites and so on, instead of building penthouse condos for bankers. There's plenty of relatively low-carbon work for us builders to do – plowing under the worst suburbs, converting the best shopping malls to retirement communities, converting McMansions to co-housing, converting Citibanks and nail salons and retail to community centers, schools, libraries, theatres and workers housing. Tearing down the commercial blight of America's cities and towns and restoring

---

[36] Ian Johnston, "Taking public transport instead of driving to work makes people happier, study suggests, *The Independent*, September 15, 2014.

[37] E.g., Tony Weiss, *The Ecological Hoofprint* (London: Zed Books 2013).

[38] E.g., Carl Honoré, *In Praise of Slowness* (New York: HarperCollins 2004).

historic architecture, urban gardens, expanding urban transit and much more. More than a century ago, long before the words ecology and slow food were coined, William Morris summed up my ideal of sensuous pleasure of social and creative work, of living better, not higher, in the following words:

> "I think that to all living things there is a pleasure in the exercise of their energies, and that even beasts rejoice in being lithe and swift and strong. But a man at work, making something which he feels will exist because he is working at it and wills it, is exercising the energies of his mind and soul as well as of his body. Memory and imagination help him as he works. Not only his own thoughts, but the thoughts of the men of past ages guide his hands; and, as a part of the human race, he creates. If we work thus we shall be men, and our days will be happy and eventful" *Signs of Change* (1896).

And we could re-train those liberated ex-bankers and Mad Men in useful skills so they can take pride in creating beauty instead of horror and they will no longer have to be ashamed to tell their kids what they do for a living. The possibilities are endless. Indeed, far from austerity and sacrifice, an eco-socialist society would free us from the endless treadmill of consumerism, the rat race of competition, the mindless drudgery of commodity production, the 24/7 work-life of multitasking, enabling us to take pleasure in unalienating work for our own enjoyment, and for the good of society, to develop our many capacities and talents in our work lives and also to shorten the work day and year so that we can enjoy the leisure once promised, but never delivered, by capitalism.

Green capitalism: the god that failed

Capitalism and the destruction of life on Earth: six theses on saving the humans

Sleepwalking to extinction

When, on May 10th 2013, scientists at Mauna Loa Observatory on the big island of Hawaii announced that global CO_2 emissions had crossed a threshold at 400 parts per million (ppm) for the first time in millions of years, a sense of dread spread around the world and not only among climate scientists. CO_2 emissions have been relentlessly climbing since Charles David Keeling first set up his tracking station near the summit of Mauna Loa Observatory in 1958 to monitor average daily global CO_2 levels. At that time, CO_2 concentrations registered 315ppm. CO_2 emissions and atmospheric concentrations have been relentlessly climbing ever since and, as the records show, temperatures rises will follow. For all the climate summits, the promises of "voluntary restraint", the carbon trading and carbon taxes, the growth of CO_2 emissions and atmospheric concentrations has not just been relentless – it has been *accelerating* in what scientists have dubbed the "Keeling Curve". In the early 1960s, CO_2ppm concentrations in the atmosphere grew by 0.7ppm per year. In recent decades, especially as China has industrialized, the growth rate has tripled to 2.1ppm per year. In just the first 17 weeks of 2013, CO_2 levels jumped by 2.74ppm compared to last year – "the biggest increase since benchmark monitoring stations high on the Hawaiian volcano of Mauna Loa began taking measurements in 1958."[1]

Carbon concentrations have not been this high since the Pliocene period, between 3 million and 5 million years ago, when global average temperatures were 3 or 4°C hotter than today, the Arctic was ice-free, sea levels were about 40m higher, jungles covered northern Canada, while Florida was under water along with coastal locations we now call New York city, London, Shanghai, Hong Kong, Sydney and many others. Crossing this threshold has fueled fears that we are fast approaching "tipping points" – melting of the subarctic tundra or thawing and releasing the vast quantities of methane in the Arctic sea bottom – that will accelerate global warming beyond any human capacity to stop it. Scripps Institute geochemist Ralph Keeling whose father Charles Keeling set up the first monitoring stations in 1958 said:

---

[1] Tom Bawden, "Carbon dioxide in atmosphere at highest level for 5 million years," *The Independent*, May 10th, 2013 at http://www.independent.co.uk/news/uk/home-news/carbon-dioxide-in-atmosphere-at-highest-level-for-5-million-years-8611673.html.

Green capitalism: the god that failed

"I wish it weren't true, but it looks like the world is going to blow through the 400-ppm level without losing a beat..."

"At this pace, we'll hit 450 ppm within a few decades."

"It feels like the inevitable march toward disaster," said Maureen E. Raymo, a scientist at the Lamont-Doherty Earth Observatory, a unit of Columbia University."[2]

Why are we marching to disaster, "sleepwalking to extinction" as the *Guardian*'s George Monbiot once put it? Why can't we slam on the brakes before we ride off the cliff to collapse? I'm going to argue here that the problem is rooted in the requirements of capitalist reproduction, that large corporations are destroying life on Earth, that they can't help themselves, they can't change or change very much, that so long as we live under this system we have little choice but to go along in this destruction, to keep pouring on the gas instead of slamming on the brakes, and that the only alternative – impossible as this may seem right now – is to overthrow this global economic system and all of the governments of the 1% that prop it up, and replace them with a global economic democracy, a radical bottom-up political democracy, an *ecosocialist civilization*. I argue that, although we are fast approaching the precipice of ecological collapse, the means to derail this trainwreck are in the making as, around the world we are witnessing a near simultaneous global mass democratic "awakening" as the Brazilians call it, almost a global uprising from Tahir Square to Zacotti Park, from Athens to Istanbul to Beijing and beyond – such as the world has never seen. To be sure, like Occupy Wall Street, these movements are still inchoate, are still mainly protesting what's wrong rather than fighting for an alternative social order. Like Occupy, they have yet to clearly and robustly answer that crucial question, "Don't like capitalism, what's your alternative?" Yet they are working on it, and they are all instinctively and radically democratic and in this lies our hope. I'm going to make my case in the form of six theses:

---

[2] Justin Gillis, "Heat-trapping gas passes milestone, raising fears," *New York Times*, May 10, 2013. Scripps Institution of Oceanography, *Scripps News*, April 23, 2013 at http://scrippsnews.ucsd.edu/Releases/?releaseID=1347.

Capitalism and destruction of life on Earth: six theses on saving the humans

1. Capitalism is, overwhelmingly, the main driver of planetary ecological collapse.

From climate change to resource overconsumption to pollution, the engine that has powered three centuries of accelerating economic development revolutionizing technology, science, culture, and human life itself is, today, a roaring out-of-control locomotive mowing down continents of forests, sweeping oceans of life, clawing out mountains of minerals, drilling, pumping out lakes of fuels, devouring the planet's last accessible resources to turn them all into "product" while destroying fragile global ecologies built up over eons of time. Between 1950 and 2000 the global human population more than doubled from 2.5 to 6 billion, but in these same decades consumption of major natural resources soared more than 6 fold on average, some much more. Natural gas consumption grew nearly 12 fold, bauxite (aluminum ore) 15 fold. And so on.[3] At current rates, Harvard biologist E.O Wilson says that:

> "...half the world's great forests have already been leveled and
> half the world's plant and animal species may be gone by the end
> of this century."

Corporations aren't necessarily evil, though plenty are diabolically evil, but they can't help themselves. They're just doing what they're supposed to do for the benefit of their shareholders. Shell Oil can't help but loot Nigeria and the Arctic and cook the climate. That's what shareholders demand.[4] BHP Billiton, Rio Tinto and other mining giants can't resist mining Australia's abundant coal and exporting it to China and India. Mining accounts for 19% of Australia's GDP and substantial employment, even as coal combustion is the single worst driver of global warming. IKEA can't help but level the forests of Siberia and Malaysia to feed the Chinese mills building its flimsy disposable furniture (IKEA is the *third largest consumer of lumber in the world*). Apple can't help it if the cost of extracting the "rare earths" it needs to make millions of new iThings each year is the destruction of the eastern Congo – violence, rape, slavery, forced induction of child soldiers, along with

---

[3] Michael T. Klare, *The Race for What's Left* (New York: Picador 2012), p. 24 Table 1.1. Jeffrey Sachs calculates that in value terms, between 1950 and 2008 the global human population rose from 2.5 to 7 billion, so less than tripled, while global GDP multiplied 8 times. *Common Wealth: Economics for a Crowded Planet* (New York: Penguin Books, 2008), p. 19.
[4] On Shell's impact on Africa see Nimo Bassey, *To Cook a Continent: Destructive Extraction and the Climate Crisis in Africa* (Cape Town: Pambazuka Press 2012).

127

poisoning local waterways.[5] Monsanto and DuPont and Syngenta and Bayer Crop Science have no choice but to wipe out bees, butterflies, birds, small farmers and extinguish crop diversity to secure their grip on the world's food supply while drenching the planet with their Roundups and Atrazines and neonicotinoids.[6] This is how giant corporations are wiping out life on Earth in the course of a routine business day. And the bigger the corporations grow, the worse the problems become.

In Adam Smith's day, when the first factories and mills produced hat pins and iron tools and rolls of cloth by the thousands, capitalist freedom to make whatever they wanted didn't much matter because they didn't have much impact on the global environment. But today, when everything is produced in the millions and billions, then trashed today and reproduced all over again tomorrow, when the planet is looted and polluted to support all this frantic and senseless growth, it matters – a lot.

The world's climate scientists tell us we're facing a *planetary emergency*. They've

[5] Delly Mawazo Sesete of Change.org, writing in the *Guardian* newspaper says, "I am originally from the North Kivu province in the eastern region of the **Democratic Republic of the Congo**, where a deadly conflict has been raging for over 15 years. While that conflict began as a war over ethnic tension, land rights and politics, it has increasingly turned to being a war of profit, with various armed groups fighting one another for control of strategic mineral reserves. Near the area where I grew up, there are mines with vast amounts of tungsten, tantalum, tin, and gold – minerals that make most consumer electronics in the world function. These minerals are part of *your* daily life. They keep your computer running so you can surf the internet. They save your high score on your Playstation. They make your cell phone vibrate when someone calls you. While minerals from the Congo have enriched your life, they have often brought violence, rape and instability to my home country. That's because those armed groups fighting for control of these mineral resources use murder, extortion and mass rape as a deliberate strategy to intimidate and control local populations, which helps them secure control of mines, trading routes and other strategic areas. Living in the Congo, I saw many of these atrocities first hand. I documented the child slaves who are forced to work in the mines in dangerous conditions. I witnessed the deadly chemicals dumped into the local environment. I saw the use of rape as a weapon. And despite receiving multiple death threats for my work, I've continued to call for peace, development and dignity in Congo's minerals trade." "Apple: time to make a conflict-free iPhone," *Guardian*, December 30, 2011 at
http://www.guardian.co.uk/commentisfree/cifamerica/2011/dec/30/apple-time-make-conflict-free-iphone. For more detail see conflictminerals.org. See also: Peter Eichstaedt, *Consuming the Congo: War and Conflict Minerals in the World's Deadliest Place* (Chicago: Lawrence Hill, 2011).
[6] Lauren McCauley, "Herbicides for GMOs driving monarch butterfly populations to 'ominous' brink," *Common Dreams*, March 14, 2013 at
http://www.commondreams.org/headline/2013/03/14-3.

been telling us since the 1990s that if we don't cut global fossil fuel greenhouse gas emissions by 80-90% below 1990 levels by 2050 we will cross critical tipping points and global warming will accelerate beyond any human power to contain it. Yet despite all the ringing alarm bells, no corporation and no government can oppose growth and, instead, every capitalist government in the world is putting pedal to the metal to accelerate growth, to drive us full throttle off the cliff to collapse. Marxists have never had a better argument against capitalism than this inescapable and apocalyptic "contradiction".

2. Solutions to the ecological crisis are blindingly obvious but we can't take the necessary steps to prevent ecological collapse because, so long as we live under capitalism, economic growth has to take priority over ecological concerns or the economy will collapse and mass unemployment will be the result.

We all know what we have to do: suppress greenhouse gas emissions. Stop overconsuming natural resources. Stop the senseless pollution of the Earth, water and atmosphere with toxic chemicals. Stop producing waste that can't be recycled by nature. Stop the destruction of biological diversity and ensure the rights of other species to flourish. We don't need any new technological breakthroughs to solve these problems. Mostly, we *just stop doing what we're doing*. But we can't stop because *we're all locked into* an economic system in which companies have to grow to compete and reward their shareholders and because *we all need the jobs.*

Take climate change:

James Hansen, the world's preeminent climate scientist, has argued that to save the humans:

> "Coal emissions must be phased out as rapidly as possible or global climate disasters will be a dead certainty... Yes, [coal, oil, gas] most of the fossil fuels must be left in the ground. That is the explicit message that the science provides.

> "Humanity treads today on a slippery slope. As we continue to pump greenhouse gases in the air, we move onto a steeper, even more slippery incline. We seem oblivious to the danger – unaware of how close we may be to a situation in which a catastrophic slip

becomes practically unavoidable, a slip where we suddenly lose all control and are pulled into a torrential stream that hurls us over a precipice to our demise."[7]

But how can we do this under capitalism? After his climate negotiators stonewalled calls for binding limits on CO_2 emissions at Copenhagen, Cancun, Cape Town and Doha, President Obama is now trying to salvage his environmental "legacy" by ordering his EPA to impose "tough" new emissions limits on existing power plants, especially coal-fired plants.[8] But this won't salvage his legacy or, more importantly, his daughters' futures, because how much difference would it make, really, if every coal-fired power plant in the U.S. shut down tomorrow *when U.S. coal producers are free to export their coal to China*, which they are doing, and when China is building another coal-fired power plan every week? The atmosphere doesn't care where the coal is burned. It only cares how much is burned. Yet how could Obama tell American mining companies *to stop mining coal*? This would be tantamount to socialism. But if we *do not stop* mining and burning coal, capitalist freedom and private property is the least we'll have to worry about.

Same with Obama's "tough" new fuel economy standards. In August 2012, Obama boasted that his new Corporate Average Fuel Economy (CAFE) standards would "double fuel efficiency" over the next 13 years to 54.5 miles per gallon by 2025, up from 28.6 mpg at present – cutting vehicle CO_2 emissions in half, so helping enormously to "save the planet". But as the Center for Biological Diversity and other critics have noted, Obama was lying. First, his so-called "tough" new CAFE standards were so full of loopholes, negotiated with Detroit, that they actually encourage *more gas-guzzling, not less.*[9] That's because the standards are based on a sliding scale according to "vehicle footprints" – the bigger the car, the less mileage it has to get to meet its "standard". So in fact Obama's "tough" standards are (surprise) custom-designed to promote what Detroit does best – produce giant

---

[7] James Hansen, *Storms of My Grandchildren* (New York: Bloomsbury 2009), pp. 70, 172-173.

[8] John M. Broder, "Obama readying emissions limits on power plants," *New York Times*, June 20, 2013.

[9] Center for Biological Diversity, "New mileage standards out of step with worsening climate crisis," press release, August 28, 2012 at http://www.biologicaldiversity.org/news/press_releases/2012/vehicle-emissions-08-28-2012.html. Also, Common Dreams staff, "New mileage standards encourage more gas-guzzling, not less: report," *Common Dreams*, August 28, 2012 at https://www.commondreams.org/headline/2012/08/28-8.

Capitalism and destruction of life on Earth: six theses on saving the humans

Sequoias, mountainous Denalis, Sierras, Yukons, Tundras and Ticonderogas, Ram Chargers and Ford F series luxury trucks, grossly obese Cadillac Escalades, soccer kid hauler Suburbans, even 8,000(!)-pound Ford Excursions – and let these gross gas hogs meet the "fleet standard". Many of these ridiculously oversized and overaccessorized behemoths are *more than twice the weight of cars and pickup trucks in the 1950s*.[10] These cars and "light" trucks are among the biggest selling vehicles in America today (GM's Sierra is #1) and they get worse gas mileage than American cars *half a century ago*. Cadillac's current Escalade gets worse mileage than its chrome bedecked tail fin-festooned land yachts of the mid-1950s![11] Little wonder Detroit applauded Obama's new CAFE standards instead of damning them as usual. Secondly, what would it matter even if Obama's new CAFE standards actually *did* double fleet mileage – when American and global vehicle fleets are *growing exponentially?* In 1950 Americans had 1 car for every 3 people. Today we have 1.2 cars for every American. In 1950 when there were about 2.6 billion humans on the planet, there were 53 million cars on the world's roads – about 1 for every 50 persons. Today, there are 7 billion people but more than 1 billion cars and industry forecasters expect there will be 2 to 2.5 billion cars on the world's roads by mid-century. China alone is expected to have a billion.[12] So, at the end of the day, incremental half measures like CAFE standards can't stop rising GHG missions. Barring some technical miracle, the only way to cut vehicle emissions is to just *stop*

---

[10] A full-size 1955 Chevrolet Bel Air weighed 3,100 pounds. A '55 Ford F-100 pickup truck also weighed 3100 (3300 with the optional V-8 motor). Even a 1955 Cadillac El Dorado, icon of fifties conspicuous consumption, only weighed 5050 pounds -- chrome bullets, tail fins and all. By comparison, today even a compact Toyota Prius weighs 3274 pounds (could it be the batteries?) while your typical full size Ford Taurus weighs more than 4,300 pounds, pickup trucks and big SUVs start at around 6,000 pounds and go up from there to 7-8000 pounds. Even though the occasional honest driver will concede he/she doesn't really "need" all this bulk and horsepower to load up at the mall, as a cheerful Texas Ford salesman noted: "We haven't found a ceiling to this luxury truck market." Joseph B. White, "Luxury pickups stray off the ranch," *Wall Street Journal*, March 21, 2012.

[11] Your typical 4,428 pound 1955 Cadillac Coupe DeVille got 12.9 mpg in city driving according to *Motor Trend Magazine* whereas your typical 2013 Cadillac Escalade gets 10mpg in the city (12mpg "combined" city and highway). Your typical 2013 Chevrolet Silverado K15 truck gets just 9 mpg hauling those heavy bags of groceries home from the mall. This is after *six decades* of Detroit fuel economy "improvements" – and Obama says Detroit is going to "double it's fleet mileage in 20 years". Good luck on that. Mileage figures for the Cadillac are from *Cadillac History 1955* at http://www.100megsfree4.com/cadillac/cad1950/cad55s.htm. For the Silverado at www.fuel economy.gov.

[12] For forecasts of China's vehicle fleet and its implications see Craig Simons, *The Devouring Dragon* (New York: St. Martins Press, 2013), p. 200.

making them – drastically suppress vehicle production, especially of the worst gas hogs. In theory, Obama could simply order GM to stop building its humongous gas guzzlers and switch to producing small economy cars. After all, the federal government *owns the company*! But of course, how could he do any such thing? Detroit lives by the mantra "big car big profit, small car small profit." Since Detroit has never been able to compete against the Japanese and Germans in the small car market, which is already glutted and nearly profitless everywhere, such an order would only doom GM to failure, if not bankruptcy (again), throw masses of workers onto the unemployment lines (and devalue the GM stock in the feds' portfolio). So given capitalism, Obama is, in fact, powerless. He's locked in to promoting the endless growth of vehicle production, even of the worst polluters – and lying about it all to the public to try to patch up his pathetic "legacy". And yet, if we don't suppress vehicle production, how can we stop rising CO_2 emissions?

In the wake of the failure of climate negotiators from Kyoto to Doha to agree on binding limits on GHG emissions, exasperated British climate scientists Kevin Anderson and Alice Bows at the Tyndall Centre, Britain's leading climate change research center, wrote in September 2012 that we need an entirely "new paradigm": government policies must "radically change" if "dangerous" climate change is to be avoided:

> "We urgently need to acknowledge that the development needs of many countries leave the rich western nations with little choice but to *immediately and severely curb their greenhouse gas emissions. . . [The]* misguided belief that commitments to avoid warming of 2 degrees C can still be realized with incremental adjustments to economic incentives. A carbon tax here, a little emissions trading there and the odd voluntary agreement thrown in for good measure will not be sufficient. . . Long-term end-point targets (for example, 80% by 2050) have no scientific basis. What governs future global temperatures and other adverse climate impacts are the emissions from yesterday, today, and those released in the next few years."[13]

And not just scientists. In its latest world energy forecast released on November 12, 2012, the International Energy Agency (IEA) warns that despite the bonanza of

---

[13] "A new paradigm for climate change," *Nature Climate Change*, Vol. 2 September 2012, pp. 639-640 (my italics).

fossil fuels now made possible by fracking, horizontal and deep-water drilling, *we can't consume them if we want to save the humans*:

> "..the climate goal of limiting global warming to 2 degrees centigrade is becoming more difficult and costly with each year that passes... No more than one-third of proven reserves of fossil fuels can be consumed prior to 2050 if the world is to achieve the 2 degree C goal..."[14]

Of course the science could be wrong about this. But so far climate scientists have consistently *underestimated* the speed and ferocity of global warming, and even prominent climate change deniers have folded their cards.[15]

"Climate emergency"

Still, it's one thing for James Hansen or Bill McKibben of 350.org to say we need to "leave the coal in the hole, the oil in the soil, the gas under the grass," to call for "severe curbs" in GHG emissions – in the abstract. *But think about what this means in our capitalist economy.* Most of us, even passionate environmental activists, don't really want to face up to the economic implications of the science we defend. That's why, if you listen to environmentalists like Bill McKibben, for example, you will get the impression that global warming is mainly driven by fossil fuel-powered electric power plants, so if we just "switch to renewables" this will solve the main problem and we can carry on with life more or less as we do now. Indeed, "green capitalism" enthusiasts like the *New York Times'* Thomas Friedman and the union-backed "green jobs" lobby look to renewable energy, electric cars and such as "the next great engine of industrial growth" – the perfect win-win solution. This is a not a solution. This is a delusion. Because greenhouse gasses are produced *across the economy* not just by or even mainly by power plants. Globally, fossil fuel-powered electricity generation accounts for 17% of GHG emissions, heating accounts for 5%,

---

[14] IEA, *World Energy Outlook 2012* Executive Summary (November 12, 2012), p. 3 at https://www.iea.org/publications/freepublications/publication/English.pdf.
[15] For a recent summary of the peer-reviewed literature see Glenn Scherer and DailyClimate.org, "Climate science predictions prove too conservative," *Scientific American December* 6, 2012 online at:
http://www.scientificamerican.com/article.cfm?id=climate-science-predictions-prove-too-conservative. Prominent ex-denier Richard A. Muller published his mea culpa on the Op-Ed page of the *New York Times:* "The conversion of a climate-change skeptic," July 28, 2012.

miscellaneous "other" fuel combustion 8.6%, industry 14.7%, industrial processes another 4.3%, transportation 14.3%, agriculture 13.6%, land use changes (mainly deforestation) 12.2%.[16] This means, for a start, that *even if we immediately replaced every fossil fuel powered electric generating plant on the planet with 100% renewable solar, wind and water power, this would only reduce global GHG emissions by around 17%.* What *this* means is that, far from launching a new green energy-powered "industrial growth" boom, barring some tech-fix miracle, the only way to impose "immediate and severe curbs" on fossil fuel production/consumption would be to impose an *EMERGENCY CONTRACTION in the industrialized countries:* drastically retrench and in some cases shut down industries, even entire sectors, across the economy and around the planet – not just fossil fuel producers but all the industries that consume them and produce GHG emissions – autos, trucking, aircraft, airlines, shipping and cruise lines, construction, chemicals, plastics, synthetic fabrics, cosmetics, synthetic fiber and fabrics, synthetic fertilizer and agribusiness CAFO operations, and many more. Of course, no one wants to hear this because, given capitalism, this would unavoidably mean mass bankruptcies, global economic collapse, depression and mass unemployment around the world. That's why in April 2013, in laying the political groundwork for his approval of the XL pipeline in some form, President Obama said:

> "The politics of this are tough... The earth's temperature probably isn't the 'number one concern' for workers who haven't seen a raise in a decade; have an underwater mortgage; are spending $40 to fill their gas tank, can't afford a hybrid car, and face other challenges."[17]

Obama wants to save the planet but *given capitalism* his "number one concern" has to be growing the economy, growing jobs. Given capitalism, today, tomorrow, next year and every year, economic growth will *always* be the overriding priority – till we barrel right off the cliff to collapse.

---

[16] World Resources Institute, *WRI Navigating the Numbers*, Table 1. pp. 4-5, at http://pdf.wri.org/navigating_numbers.pdf.
[17] The Hill blog http://thehill.com/blogs/e2-wire/e2-wire/291787-obama-on-climate-change-the-politics-of-this-are-tough.

Capitalism and destruction of life on Earth: six theses on saving the humans

The necessity of denial and delusion

There's no *technical* solution to this problem and no *market* solution either. In a very few cases – electricity generation is the main one – a broad shift to renewables could indeed sharply reduce fossil fuel emissions in that sector. But if we just use "clean" "green" energy to power more growth, consume ever more natural resources, then we solve nothing and would still be headed to collapse. Agriculture is another sector in which reliance on fossil fuels could be sharply reduced – by abandoning synthetic fertilizers and pesticides and switching to organic farming. And there's no downside there – just the resistance of the agribusiness industrial complex. But for the rest of the economy – mining, manufacturing, transportation, chemicals, most services (e.g. construction, tourism, advertising, etc.), there are no such easy substitutes. Take transportation. There are no solar powered ships or airplanes or trains on anyone's drawing boards. Producing millions of electric cars instead of millions of gasoline-powered cars, as I explained elsewhere, would be just as ecologically destructive and polluting, if in somewhat different ways, even if they were all run on solar power.[18] Substituting biofuels for fossil fuels in transportation just creates different but no less environmentally destructive problems: converting farm land to raise biofuel feedstock pits food production against fuels. Converting rainforests, peatlands, savannas or grasslands to produce biofuels releases more CO_2 into the atmosphere than the fossil fuels they replace and accelerates species extinction.[19] More industrial farming means more demand for water, synthetic fertilizers and pesticides. And so on. *Cap and trade* schemes can't cut fossil fuel emissions because, as I also explained elsewhere[20] business understands, even if some environmentalists do not, that "dematerialization" is a fantasy, that there's no win-win tech solution, that capping emissions means cutting growth. Since cutting growth is unacceptable to business, labor, and governments, cap and trade has been abandoned everywhere.[21]

Carbon taxes can't stop global warming either because they *do not* cap emissions. That's why fossil fuel execs like Rex Tillerson, CEO of ExxonMobil (the largest private oil company in the world) and Paul Anderson, CEO of Duke Energy (the

---

[18] See my "Green capitalism," *op cit.* pp. 131-133.
[19] Eg. David Biello, "The false promise of biofuels," *Scientific American*, August 2011, pp. 59-65.
[20] Smith, "Green capitalism," *op cit.* pp. 117-122.
[21] *Ibid.*

largest electric utility in the U.S.) *support* carbon taxes. They understand that carbon taxes would add something to the cost of doing business, like other taxes, but they pose no limit, no "cap" on growth.[22] Exxon predicts that, carbon tax or no carbon tax, by 2040 global demand for energy is going to grow by 35%, 65% in the developing world and nearly all of this is going to be supplied by fossil fuels. ExxonMobil is not looking to "leave the oil in the soil" as a favor to Bill McKibben and the humans. ExxonMobil is looking to pump it and burn it all as fast as possible to enrich its shareholders.[23]

James Hansen, Bill McKibben, Barack Obama – and most of us really, don't want to face up to the economic implications of the need to put the brakes on growth and fossil fuel-based overconsumption. We all "need" to live in denial, and believe in delusions that carbon taxes or some tech fix will save us because we all know that capitalism has to grow or we'll all be out of work. And the thought of replacing capitalism seems so impossible, especially given the powers arrayed against change. But what's the alternative? In the not-so-distant future, this is all going to come to a screeching halt one way or another – either we seize hold of this out-of-control locomotive and wrench down this overproduction of fossil fuels, or we ride this train right off the cliff to collapse.

Same with resource depletion

We in the industrialized "consumer economies" are not just overconsuming fossil fuels. We're overconsuming *everything*. From fish to forests, minerals to metals, oil to fresh water, we're consuming the planet like there's no tomorrow.[24] Ecological

---

[22] *Ibid.*

[23] ExxonMobil, *The Outlook for Energy: A View to 2040* (December 2012) at http://exxonmobil.com/corporate/files/news_pub_eo2013.pdf. See also, Jon Queally, "BP's Big Plan: Burn it. Burn it all," *Common Dreams*, January 17, 2013 at https://www.commondreams.org/headline/2013/01/17.

[24] E.g. John Parnell, "World on course to run out of water, warns Ban Ki-moon," *Guardian*, May 22, 22013. Gaia Vince, "How the world's oceans could be running out of fish," *BBC News Online*, September 12, 2012 at http://www.bbc.com/future/story/20120920-are-we-running-out-of-fish. And as tropical forests, biodiversity is being sacrificed even in nominally protected areas at an alarming rate. See William F. Laurance et al. "Averting biodiversity collapse in tropical forest protected areas," *Nature*, no. 489 September 12, 2012 pp. 290-294. "Widespread local 'extinctions' in tropical forest 'remnants'" Also, *ScienceDaily*, August 14, 2012 at http://www.sciencedaily.com/releases/2012/08/120814213404.htm. On minerals and oil see Michael T. Klare, *The Race for What's Left* (New York: Picador 2012).

Capitalism and destruction of life on Earth: six theses on saving the humans

"footprint" scientists tell us that we in the industrialized nations are now consuming resources and sinks at the rate of 1.5 planets per year, that is, we're using natural resources like fish, forests, water, farmland, and so on at half-again the rate that nature can replenish them.[25] According to the World Bank, the wealthiest 10% of the world's people account for almost 60% of consumption expenditures and the top 20% account for more than 76% of global consumption whereas the bottom 40% of the world's population account for just 5%. Even the bottom 70% of the world's population account for barely 15.3% of global consumption expenditures.[26] Needless to say, those 70 percent want and deserve a higher material standard of living. Yet if the whole world were to achieve this *by consuming like Americans*, we would need something like 5 more planets worth of natural resources and sinks for all of that.[27] *Think what this means.*

Take the case of China. Columbia University's Earth Policy Institute predicts that if China keeps growing by around 8% per year, its current rate, Chinese average per capita consumption will reach current U.S. level by around 2035. But to provide the natural resources for China's 1.3+ billion to consume like America's 330 million, the Chinese, roughly 20% of the world's population, will consume as much oil *as the entire world* consumes today, they will consume 69% of current world grain production, 62% of the current world meat production, 63% of current world coal consumption, 35% of current world steel consumption, 84% of current world paper consumption. (See Table 1.) Well, where on Earth are the Chinese going to find the resources (not to mention sinks) to support all this consumption? China certainly doesn't have the resources. That's why the Chinese are buying up the planet. And that's just China. What about the other four-fifths of humanity? What are *they* going to consume in 2035?

---

[25] Ecological "footprint" studies show that today humanity uses the equivalent of 1.5 planets to provide the resources we use and absorb our waste. This means it now takes the Earth one year and six months to regenerate what we use in a year. Moderate UN scenarios suggest that if current population and consumption trends continue, by the 2030s, we will need the equivalent of two Earths to support us. And of course, we only have one. Turning resources into waste faster than waste can be turned back into resources puts us in global ecological "overshoot" depleting the very resources on which human life and biodiversity depend. See the Global Footprint Network at
http://www.footprintnetwork.org/en/index.php/GFN/page/world_footprint/.
[26] World Bank, *2008 World Development Indicators*, p. 4 Table 1J at
http://data.worldbank.org/sites/default/files/wdi08.pdf.
[27] Worldwatch Institute, *2010 State of the World: Transforming Cultures From Consumerism to Sustainability* (New York: Norton, 2010) pp. 3-7ff. Also Alan Durning, *How Much is Enough?* (New York: Norton 1992). Avatar.

Table 1: Annual Consumption of Key Resources in China and U.S., Latest Year, with Projections for China to 2035, Compared to Current World Production

Commodity	Unit	Consumption Latest Year U.S.	China	Projected Consumption* 2035 China	Production Latest Year World
Grain	Million Tons	338	424	1,505	2,191
Meat	Million Tons	37	73	166	270
Oil	Million Barrels per Day	19	9	85	86
Coal	Million Tons of Oil Equiv.	525	1,714	2,335	3,731
Steel	Million Tons	102	453	456	1,329
Fertilizer	Million Tons	20	49	91	214
Paper	Million Tons	74	97	331	394

Note: Projected Chinese consumption in 2035 is calculated assuming per-capita consumption will be equal to the current U.S. level, based on projected GDP growth of 8 percent annually. Latest year figures for grain, oil, coal, fertilizer and paper are from 2008. Latest year figures for meat and steel are from 2010.

Source: Earth Policy Institute.

China's communist-capitalist environmental nightmare

As Beijing was choking on smog in the winter of 2013, Deutsche Bank analysts gloomily concluded that, barring extreme reforms, Chinese coal consumption and increased car ownership will push **pollution** levels 70% higher by 2025. They say that even if China's economy slowed to 5% growth each year, its annual coal consumption would still rise to 6 billion tons (5.4 tonnes) by 2022, from the current 3.8 billion tons. Car ownership is expected to increase over the years to 400 million in 2030 from the current 90 million. With those two figures, it will be very difficult for the government to reduce the national average of PM2.5 (air pollution) low enough not to enter the bloodstream. The current national average is 75 micrograms per cubic meter. In January, PM2.5 levels in Beijing reached 900 micrograms per cubic meter.

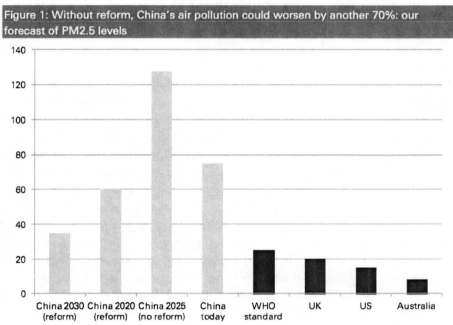

Figure 1: Without reform, China's air pollution could worsen by another 70%: our forecast of PM2.5 levels

Source: Deutsche Bank estimates, WHO, NASA

Already, as resource analyst Michael Klare reviews in his latest book *The Race for What's Left*, around the world existing reserves of oil, minerals and other resources "are being depleted at a terrifying pace and will be largely exhausted in the not-too-distant future". This is driving miners and drillers to the ends of the Earth, the bottom of oceans, to the arctic. We're running out of planet to plunder so fast that serious people like Google's Larry Page and Eric Schmidt have partnered with film director James Cameron to make life imitate art, to explore the possibility of mining asteroids and near planets. *Avatar* – the perfect capitalist solution to resource exhaustion (but the Marines will be Chinese).[28]

---

[28] Michael T. Klare, *The Race for What's Left*, p. 12 (my italics). AP, "Tech tycoons in asteroid mining venture," *Guardian*, April 20, 2012.

Green capitalism: the god that failed

"Wild facts" and unquestioned assumptions

In mainstream discourse it is taken as an absolutely *unquestioned given* by scientists like James Hansen, environmentalists like George Monbiot, not to mention CEOs and presidents, that demand for everything must *grow infinitely,* that economies must grow *forever.* That's why Hansen, Monbiot, James Lovelock and others tell us that, Fukishima notwithstanding, we "have to" *go nuclear* for energy production. In their view, the human population is headed for 9 billion, all these billions want to consume like Americans so we will need more power for their washing machines, air conditioners, iPads, TVs and (electric) SUVs, we can't burn more fossil fuels to produce this power because it will cook the planet, renewables are great but can't reliably and everywhere meet relentlessly growing "base load" demand for electricity 24/7 – *therefore* they tell us, we have "no choice" but to turn to nuclear power. (Besides, what could go wrong with the "newest" "safest" "fourth generation" reactors? What indeed?)[29] But not one of these people stops to ask the obvious question, which is *where are all the resources going to come from to support insatiable consumption on a global scale?* In the capitalist lexicon there is no concept of "too much". The word "overconsumption" cannot be found in Econ. 101 text books except as a temporary market aberration, soon to be erased as "perfect competition" matches supply to demand and shortages and surpluses vanish down the gullet of the consumer. The fact that we live on one small planet with finite resources and sinks is just beyond the capitalist imagination *because,* as Herman Daly used to say, the "wild facts" of environmental reality demolish their underlying premise of the viability of endless growth on a finite planet. So inconvenient facts must be *denied,* suppressed or ignored. And they are. When, on May 10th 2013, climate scientists announced the latest "wild fact" that the level of heat-trapping CO_2 concentrations in the atmosphere had passed the long-feared milestone of 400ppm, an event fraught with ominous consequences for us all, this was met with total silence from the world's economic and political elites. President Obama was busy preparing his own announcement – that he was clearing the way

---

[29] Hansen, *Storms,* chapter 9. Independent Voices: "James Lovelock: Nuclear power is the only green solution," *Independent,* May 24, 2004 at
http://www.independent.co.uk/voices/commentators/james-lovelock-nuclear-power-is-the-only-green-solution-6169341.html. George Monbiot the Guardian columnist has argued this in many venues but see in particular his blog piece: "The moral case for nuclear power," August 8, 2011 at http://www.monbiot.com/2011/08/08/the-moral-case-for-nuclear-power/. Also, Ted Nordhaus and Michael Shellenberger, "Going green? Then go nuclear," *Wall Street Journal* op-ed, May 23, 2013.

for *accelerated natural-gas exports* by approving a huge new $10 billion Freeport LNG facility in Texas. Obama's Deptartment of Energy gave Freeport LNG the green light because it "found the prospective benefits from exporting energy outweighed concerns about possible downsides". No surprise there. Freeport LNG chief Michael Smith wasn't anticipating downsides or any change in Obama's priorities. He said: "I hope this means that more facilities will get approval in due time, sooner than later. The country needs these exports for jobs, for trade, and for geopolitical reasons..." [30] That's why, even though, at some repressed level, most Americans understand that fracking the planet is disastrous, even suicidal for their own children in the long run, yet still *for the present* they have to make the mortgage payments, fill the gas tank, and so they have little choice but to live in denial and support fracking.[31] And so we go, down the slippery slope.

No one stops to ask "what's it all for?" Why do we "need" all this energy? Why do we "need" all the stuff we produce with all this energy? It's high time we start asking this question. Economists tell us that two-thirds of America's own economy is geared to producing "consumer" goods and services. To be sure, we need food, clothing, housing, transportation, and energy to run all this. But as Vance Packard astutely observed half a century ago, most of what corporations produce today is produced not for the needs of people but *for the needs of corporations to sell to people.* From the ever-more obscene and pointless vanities of ruling class consumption – the Bentleys and Maseratis, the Bergdorf Goodman designer collections, the penthouses and resorts and estates and yachts and jets, to the endless waste stream of designed-in obsolescence-driven mass market fashions, cosmetics, furniture, cars, "consumer electronics" the obese 1000-calorie Big Macs with fries, the obese and overaccesorized SUVs and "light trucks", the obese and ever-growing McMansions for ever-smaller middle class families, the whole-house central air conditioning, flat screen TVs in every room, iThings in every hand, H&M disposable "fast fashion" too cheap to bother to clean, [32] the frivolous and

---

[30] Keith Johnson and Ben Lefebvre, "U.S. approves expanded gas exports," *Wall Street Journal*, May 18th, 2013.

[31] John Vogel, "Methane gas 'fracking:' 3 polls show public leaning to toward yes," *American Agriculturalist*, April 9, 2013 at http://farmprogress.com/story-methane-gas-fracking-3-polls-show-public-leaning-toward-yes-9-96948. Karen DeWitt, "Poll shows increased support for fracking," *North Country Public Radio*, September 13, 2012 at http://www.northcountrypublicradio.org/news/story/20474/20120913/poll-shows-increased-support-for-fracking.

[32] Clothing designer Eliza Starbuck says of ultra-cheap producers like H&M "It's throwaway fashion or 'trashion.' If their prices are that cheap that people are throwing their disposable

astonishingly polluting jet and cruise ship vacations everywhere (even *Nation* magazine cruises with Naomi Klein!), and all the retail malls, office complexes, the packaging, shipping industries, the junk mail/magazine/catalog sales companies, the advertising, banking and credit card "industries" that keep this perpetual consumption machine humming along, not to mention the appalling waste of the arms industry, which is just total deliberate waste and destruction, the vast majority – I would guess *at least three quarters* of all the goods and services we produce today *just do not need to be produced at all. It's all just a resource-hogging, polluting* waste. My parents lived passably comfortable working class lives in the 1940s and 50s without half this stuff and they weren't living in caves. We could all live happier, better, more meaningful lives without all this junk – and we *do not* need ever-more energy, solar or otherwise, to produce it. We could shut down all the coal-powered electric generators around the world, most of which, especially in China, are currently dedicated to powering the production of superfluous and disposable junk we don't need and replace them with – *nothing*. How's *that* for a sustainable solution? Same with nuclear. Since the 1960s, Japan built 54 nuclear power plants. But these were built not so much to provide electricity for the Japanese (their population is falling) as to power Japan's mighty manufacturing export engine producing all those disposable Gameboys and TVs and Toyotas and Hondas the world does not need and can no longer afford to "consume".

---

income at them – only to find that the clothes fall apart on the hangers after a wash or two – they're just creating garbage. . . It takes such a huge amount of human energy and textile fibers, dyes, and chemicals to create even poor quality clothes. They may be offering fashions at a price anyone can afford in an economic crunch, but they're being irresponsible about what happens to the goods after the consumers purchase them." Jasmin Malik Chua, "Is H&M's new lower-priced clothing encouraging disposable fashion?" *ecouterre*, September 28, 2010 at: http://www.ecouterre.com/is-h-m-new-lower-priced-clothing-encouraging-disposable-fashion/2/. And H&M takes "disposable" literally. As the *New York Times* reported in 2012, H&M's employees systematically slash and rip perfectly good unsold clothes before tossing them in dumpsters at the back of the chain's 34th St. store in Manhattan – to make sure they can't be sold but thus adding pointlessly to landfills rather than donating them to charity. *It is little remarked that capitalism is the first economic system in which perfectly serviceable, even brand new goods from clothes to automobiles (recall the "cash for clunkers" rebates) are deliberately destroyed so as to promote production of their replacements.* I'll explore this interesting theme further elsewhere. See Jim Dwyer, "A clothing clearance where more than just the prices are slashed," *New York Times,* January 5, 2010. Also, Ann Zimmerman and Neil Shah, "Taste for cheap clothes fed Bangladesh boom," *Wall Street Journal*, May 13, 2013.

Capitalism and destruction of life on Earth: six theses on saving the humans

Endless growth or repair, rebuild, upgrade, recycle?

So, for example, at the risk of sounding ridiculous, we don't really *need* a global automobile industry. At least we don't need an industry cranking out hundreds of millions of new cars every year because the industry is built on the principle of designed-in obsolescence, on insatiable repetitive consumption, on advertising and "cash for clunkers" programs to push you to crush your perfectly good present car for a "new" "improved", "bigger" "more luxurious" model that is, in reality, trivially different, sometimes even inferior to the one you just junked. What we need is a different approach to transportation. To build a sustainable transportation system, we would have to divert most resources from auto production to public transportation, trains, busses, and bicycling. But of course bikes and public transport aren't feasible everywhere and for every task, particularly for those who live in the suburbs or the country or in the mostly rural developing world. So we would still need some cars and trucks – but many fewer if we "degrow" the economy to produce just what we need instead of for profit. As the VW ads below point out, properly designed and engineered cars can be sturdy but simple, economical to drive, easily, even DIY serviceable and repairable, *perpetually rebuildable and upgradable as needed.* I'm not suggesting an ecosocialist society should produce *this particular* "peoples' car". We need something with modern safety features. But to the extent that we would need cars in a sustainable society, we could save immense resources and GHG emissions by producing massively fewer cars and keep them running for decades if not practically forever. Reducing global car production to something like, say 10 percent of current production – *and sharing those* – would not only save vast resources and eliminate massive pollution but also free up labor and resources for other uses, let us shorten the working day – and take longer vacations!

The same goes for all kinds of industries.

Apple could easily build you iPhones and iMacs, in classic timeless designs that could last for decades, that could be easily be upgraded. This would save mountains of resources not to mention the lives Congolese kids and Foxconn assembly workers. But how much profit is there in that? Apple could never justify such a humane and environmentally rational approach to its shareholders because shareholders (who are several stages removed from the "sourcing" process and don't really care to know about it) are capitalist rationally looking to maximize returns on their portfolios, not to maximize the lifespan of the company's products, let alone

143

the lifespan of Congolese or Chinese people. So to this end, you have to be convinced that your G4 phone is not *good enough,* that you "need" an iPhone5 because you need a phone that streams movies, that talks to you and more, and next year you will need an iPhone6. And even if you own an iPad3 you will soon "need" an iPad4, plus an iPad Mini, and how will you live without iTV? This incessant, exponentially growing demand for the latest model of disposable electronic gadgets is destroying societies and the environment from Congo to China and beyond.

IKEA could easily manufacture beautifully designed, high quality, sturdy and durable furniture that could last a lifetime, that could be handed down to your children or passed on friends or antique shops for others. That would save a Siberia's worth of trees, lakes of toxic dyes and finishes, and vast quantities of other resources. But why would they do that? IKEA is not in business to make furniture or save the planet. IKEA is in the business to make money. As Ingvar Kamprad, founder and CEO of IKEA, long ago discovered, the way to maximize profits (besides employing semi-slave forced labor in Stalinist regimes and moving his "Swedish" company from high-tax Sweden to low-tax Holland and Switzerland)[33] is to relentlessly cheapen production by, among other tactics, building flat pack disposable particleboard furniture in accordance with the IRON LAW OF MARKETING to sell "the cheapest construction for the briefest interval the buying public will tolerate" so IKEA can chop down more Siberian birch trees and sell you the same shoddy $59 bookcase all over again that will last you as long as the first one did – perhaps a bit longer this time if you don't actually load many books of those flimsy shelves. As an IKEA commercial, directed by Spike Jonze, tells us: "an old lamp (or bookcase or table) doesn't have any feelings; any piece of furniture can and should be replaced at any time." The ad, and the whole IKEA approach, suggests that objects have no lasting meaning or value. They're disposable; when we tire of them, we should just throw them out.[34] This is how IKEA got to be the third largest consumer of wood in the world, most of it from East Europe and the Russian Siberia where, according to the World Bank, half of all logging is illegal even by the Russian kleptocracy's standards of legality. IKEA's wholly-owned Swedish

---

[33] Juan O. Tamayo, "STASI records show Cuba deal included IKEA furniture, antiques, rum and guns," *McClatchy Newspapers,* May 9, 2012. James Angelos, "IKEA regrets use of East German prisoners," *Wall Street Journal,* November 16, 2012.

[34] I am quoting here from Stephanie Zacharek's excellent "IKEA is as bad as Wal-Mart," *Salon.com,* July 12, 2009: 12:11PM at
http://www.salon.com/2009/07/12/cheap/singleton reviewing Ellen Ruppel Shell, *Cheap: The High cost of Discount Culture* (New York: Penguin, 2009), chapter 6.

subsidiary **Swedwood** has even been condemned by Russian nature conservancy organizations and the Global Forest Coalition for clear-cutting 1,400 acres a year of 200-600 year old old-growth forest near the Finnish border, a process that "is having deep ramifications on invaluable forest ecosystems."[35] This is how IKEA's business plan based on endless "repetitive consumption" is wiping out life on Earth. Here again, the capitalist freedom to make such junk wouldn't matter – if it weren't costing the earth.[36]

Given capitalism, there's no way to "incentivize" GM to stop producing new cars every year, IKEA to stop making its disposable furniture, Apple to stop pushing you to lose your iPhone5 and buy a 6. That's what they're invested in. Companies can't change, or change much, because it's too costly, too risky, shareholders won't allow it. And given capitalism, most workers, most of the time, have no choice but to support all this suicidal overconsumption because if we all stop shopping to save the planet today, we'd all be out of work tomorrow. Ask your nearest 6-year old what's wrong with this picture.

Capitalism and délastage in the richest country of poor people in the world

Yet even as corporations are plundering the planet to overproduce stuff we don't need, huge social, economic and ecological needs – housing, schools, infrastructure, health care, environmental remediation – go unmet, even in the industrialized world, while most of third world lacks even basic sanitation, clean water, schools, health care, ecological restoration, not to mention jobs.[37] After 300 years of capitalist "development" the gap between rich and poor has never been wider: today, almost half the world, more than 3 billion people, live on less than $2.50 a day, 80% of humanity lives on less than $10 a day. This while the world's richest 1% own 40% of the world's wealth. The richest 10% own 85% of total global assets and half the world barely owns 1% of global wealth. And these gaps have only widened over

---

[35] Ida Karisson, "IKEA products made from 600-year old trees," Inter Press Service, May 29, 2012 Common Dreams.org at
https://www.commondreams.org/headline/2012/05/29-1.
[36] E.g., Fred Pearce, "Ikea—you can't build a green reputation with a flatpack DIY manual, the *Guardian,* April 2, 2009. Also: Greenpeace, *Slaughtering the Amazon*, July 2009 at
http://www.greenpeace.org/international/en/publications/reports/slaughtering-the-amazon/.
Alfonso Daniels, "Battling Siberia's devastating illegal logging trade," *BBC news online*, November 27, 2009.
[37] Michael Davis, *Planet of Slums* (London: Verso 2006).

time.[38] In Congo, one of the lushest, most fertile countries on the planet, with untold natural wealth in minerals, lumber, tropical crops and more, its resources are plundered every day to support gross overconsumption in the North while poverty, hunger and malnutrition are so widespread that Congo is now listed dead last on the 2011 Global Hunger Index, a measure of malnutrition and child nutrition compiled by the International Food Policy Research Institute. While European and American corporations loot its copper and cobalt and coltran for iPhones and such, *half the population eats only once a day and a quarter less than that.* Things have reached such a state that in places like the capital Kinshasha, parents can only afford to feed their children *every other day.* Congolese call it *"délastage"* – an ironic take-off on the rolling electrical blackouts that routinely hit first one neighborhood then the next. In this context it means "Today we eat! Tomorrow we don't." "On some days," one citizen told a *New York Times* reporter, "some children eat, others do not. On other days, all the children eat, and the adults do not. Or vice versa."[39] This, in the 21st century, in one of the resource-richest countries on Earth.

Contraction or collapse

If there's no market mechanism to stop plundering the planet then, again, what alternative is there but to impose an *emergency contraction* on resource consumption? This doesn't mean we would have to de-industrialize and go back to riding horses and living in log cabins. But it does mean that we would have to abandon the "consumer economy" – shut down all kinds of unnecessary, wasteful, and polluting industries from junk food to cruise ships, disposable Pampers to disposable H&M clothes, disposable IKEA furniture, endless new model cars, phones, electronic games, the lot. Plus all the banking, advertising, junk mail, most retail, etc. We would have completely redesign production to replace "fast junk food" with healthy, nutritious, fresh "slow food," replace "fast fashion" with "slow

---

[38] World Bank Development Indicators 2008, cited in Anup Shah, Poverty and stats, *Global Issues* January 7, 2013 at http://www.globalissues.org/article/26/poverty-facts-and-stats#src1. World Institute for Development Economics Research of the UN cited in James Randerson, "World's richest 1% own 40% of all wealth, UN report discovers," *Guardian*, December 6, 2006. As for trends, in 1979 the richest 1% in the U.S. earned 33.1% more than the bottom 20%. In 2000 the wealthiest 1% made 88.5% more than the poorest 20%. In the Third World, polarization has grown even worse, especially in China which in 1978 had the world's most equal incomes while today, it has the most unequal incomes of any large society. Who says capitalism doesn't work?!
[39] Adam Nossiter, "For Congo children, food today means none tomorrow," *New York Times*, January 3, 2012.

fashion," bring back mending, alterations, and local tailors and shoe repairmen. We would have to completely redesign production of appliances, electronics, housewares, furniture and so on to be durable and long-lived as possible. Bring back appliance repairmen and such. We would have to abolish the throwaway disposables industries, the packaging and plastic bag industrial complex, bring back refillable bottles and the like. We would have to design and build housing to last for centuries, to be as energy efficient as possible, to be reconfigurable and shareable. We would have to vastly expand public transportation to curb vehicle use but also build those we do need to last and be shareable like Zipcar or Paris's municipally-owned "Autolib" shared electric cars. *These are the sorts of things we would have to do to if we really want to stop overconsumption and save the world.* All these changes are simple, self-evident, no great technical challenge. They just require a completely different kind of economy, an economy geared to producing what we need while conserving resources for future generations of humans and for other species with which we share this planet.

3. If capitalism can't help but destroy the world, then what alternative is there but to nationalize and socialize most of the economy and plan it directly, even plan most of the global industrial economy?

With 7 billion of us humans crowded on one small planet running out of resources, with cities disappearing under vast clouds of pollution, with the glaciers and ice caps melting, and species going extinct by the hour, we desperately need a PLAN to avert ecological collapse. We need a comprehensive *global plan*, a number of *national or regional plans*, and *a multitude of local plans* – and we need to coordinate them all. When climate scientists call on governments to cut CO_2 emissions to stay within a global "carbon budget" if we want to keep a liveable planet, isn't that in effect calling for "planning," indeed, planning on a global scale? When governments pump money into research projects like nuclear power or biotech or the internet or clean energy projects, isn't that planning? When scientists say that we need to massively reduce and limit consumption of oil, coal, trees, fish, all kinds of scarce resources, or stop dumping chemicals in the world's oceans – isn't that in effect physical planning and rationing? And don't we want that? Indeed, since we all breathe the same air, live in the same biosphere, don't we really want and need something like a "one-world government" at least on environmental issues? How else can we regulate humanity's collective impact on the global biosphere? How else can we reorganize

147

and reprioritize the economy in the common interest and environmental rationality except in a mostly planned and mostly publicly owned economy?

What would we have to do to save the humans?

If we want a sustainable economy, one that "meets the needs of present generations without compromising the ability of future generations to meet their needs," then we would have to do *at least some or all of the following:*

1. Put the brakes on out-of-control growth in the global North – retrench or shut down unnecessary, resource-hogging, wasteful, polluting industries like fossil fuels, autos, aircraft and airlines, shipping, chemicals, bottled water, processed foods, unnecessary pharmaceuticals, and so on. Abolish luxury goods production, the fashions, jewelry, handbags, mansions, Bentleys, yachts, private jets etc. Abolish the manufacture of disposable, throw away and "repetitive consumption" products. All these consume resources we're running out of, resources which other people on the planet desperately need, and which our children and theirs will need.
2. Discontinue harmful industrial processes like industrial agriculture, industrial fishing, logging, mining and so on.
3. Close down many services – the banking industry, Wall Street, the credit card, retail, PR and advertising "industries" built to underwrite and promote all this overconsumption. I'm sure most of the people working in these so-called industries would rather be doing something else, something useful, creative and interesting and personally rewarding with their lives. They deserve that chance.
4. Abolish the military-surveillance-police state industrial complex, and all its manufactures as this is just a total waste whose only purpose is global domination, terrorism and destruction abroad and repression at home. We can't build decent societies anywhere when so much of social surplus is squandered on such waste.
5. Reorganize, restructure, reprioritize production and build the products we do need to be as durable *and shareable* as possible.
6. Steer investments into things society *does* need like renewable energy, organic farming, public transportation, public water systems, ecological remediation, public health, quality schools and other currently unmet needs.
7. Deglobalize trade to produce what can be produced locally, trade what can't be produced locally, to reduce transportation pollution and revive local producers.

8. Equalize development the world over by shifting resources out of useless and harmful production in the North and into developing the South, building basic infrastructure, sanitation systems, public schools, health care, and so on.

9. Devise a rational approach to eliminate and/or control waste and toxins as much as possible.

10. Provide equivalent jobs for workers displaced by the retrenchment or closure of unnecessary or harmful industries, not just the unemployment line, not just because otherwise, workers cannot support the industrial we and they need to save ourselves.

"Necessary", "unnecessary" and who's the "decider"?

Now we might all agree that we have to cut "overconsumption" to save the humans. But who's to say what's "necessary" and "unnecessary?" How do we decide what to cut? And who's to decide? Under capitalism goods and services are rationed by the market. But that's not sustainable because the market can't restrain consumption, the market can only accelerate consumption. So we need a non-market approach. I don't claim to have all the answers. This is a big question and I'm sure there are others better qualified than me to figure out solutions. But I would think the short answer has to be a combination of *planning, rationing and democracy.* I don't see why that's so hard. The U.S. government planned significant parts of the U.S. economy during World War II and rationed many goods and services. And we managed just fine. Actually, far from suffering unduly, Americans took pride in conservation and sharing. Besides, what's the alternative? What other choice do we have? There are only so many ways to organize a modern industrial economy.

The challenges of physically planning the world economy in the interests of the 99% instead of for the 1% – reorganizing and reprioritizing the world economy to provide every person sufficient, nutritious, safe and delicious food, providing every human with high quality, pleasurable, and aesthetically appealing housing, consolidating our cities to maximize the feasibility of public transportation, building great schools to enable every student to reach her or his fullest potential, providing top-notch health care for everyone on the planet, reorganizing and reprioritizing work so that everyone can find constructive, enjoyable, interesting, challenging and rewarding work, work that's rewarding in many ways beyond simple remuneration, providing fun, enlightening and inspiring entertainment, reducing the workday so people can actually have time to enjoy themselves and pursue other pleasures, while, not least, how to limit our collective human impact on the planet so as to leave space and resources to all the other wonderful life forms with which we have the pleasure of sharing this unique and amazing planet – all these are no doubt big challenges. They're very big *political* challenges. But they're not an *economic* challenge. This is not Soviet Russia in 1917. I'm not proposing Maoist austerity. Today, there's more than enough wealth and productive capacity to provide every person on Earth a *very satisfactory material standard of living*. Even more than half a century ago, Gandhi was right to say then that "there's more than enough wealth for man's need but never enough for some men's greed." I doubt that it would even be much of a *technical* challenge. Google's Larry Page predicts that the virtually everyone in the world will have access to the internet by 2020. Quantifying human needs, global resources, and global agricultural and industrial capacities is, I would think, a fairly pedestrian task for today's computers, with all their algorithms.

Planning can't work?

Right-wing economists like Milton Friedman denied the very possibility of planning any economy, equating all planning with Stalinism. I don't buy that. The question is, planning by whom, for whom? Stalinist central planning was planning from the top down, *by and for* a totalitarian bureaucracy. It completely shut out workers and the rest of society from the planning process. So it's hardly surprising that planning didn't work so well in the USSR. But I don't see what that tells us about the potentials of planning from the bottom up, of democratic planning. Besides, capitalists *indirectly* plan the national and global economies all the time. They meet every year at Davos to shape the world market for their benefit. They conspire to privatize medicine, schools, public transportation, force us to buy "their" water or eat GMO foods. They use the IMF and World Bank to shackle countries with debt, then open them up to U.S. corporate takeover. They've been using their states for centuries to expropriate peasants and tribes, even to exterminate them when necessary as in the Americas, to steal and privatize common lands, break up pre-capitalist societies, re-organize, re-plan whole continents to set up the right "business climate" for capital accumulation. Late developers like Japan and South Korea used their state-backed MITIs and Chaebols to hothouse their own industries, protect them, and strategically plan their integration into the world market. Capitalists are *very good* at planning – for their own interests. So why can't we plan the economy for *our own interests?*

Capitalism and destruction of life on Earth: six theses on saving the humans

Government "can't pick winners"?

Disengenuous capitalist apologists, like the *Wall Street Journal,* are quick to condemn any perceived government funded "failures" like the recent bankruptcy of solar startup Solyndra Corporation bankrolled by the Obama administration as proof that "government can't pick winners". But Solyndra didn't fail because solar is a losing technology. It failed because, ironically, capitalist Solyndra could not compete against lower-cost, state-owned, state-directed, and state-subsidized competitors in *China.* Besides, since when do capitalists have a crystal ball? CEOs and corporate boards bet on "loser" technologies and products all the time. Look at the recent collapse of electric car startup Fisker Automotive, or Better Place, the Israeli electric vehicle charging/battery swapping stations venture.[40] These join a long list of misplaced private bets from Sony's Betamax to Polaroid, Ford's Edsel, Tucker Autonobilie, DeLorean Motor Company and all the way back to White Star Lines Titanic and the Tulip Mania. CEOs and boards not only pick losing technology and products, they also lose money for their shareholders and even drive perfectly successful companies into bankruptcy every day: Jamie Dimon at JP Morgan, Lehman Brothers, Washington Mutual, Enron, World Com, Pan Am, SwissAir and on and on. Who knows if Zipcar or Tesla Motors will ever make money? Government-backed Solyndra lost $500 million. But when Jamie Dimon lost $12 *billion* for JP Morgan, I don't recall the *Journal* howling that capitalists "can't pick winners". When Enron collapsed, I don't recall hearing any blanket condemnation of the "inevitable incompetence" of the private sector. Hypocrisy is stock and trade of capitalists, lazy media, and fact-averse capitalist economists who want to make the facts fit their simple-minded model – no matter the truth. That's why it's entirely in character that the *Wall Street Journal* has never bothered to applaud government when it picked *indisputable winners:* when government-funded, government-directed applied research produced nuclear weapons, nuclear energy, radar, rockets, the jet engine, the transistor, the microchip, the internet, GPS and crucial breakthroughs in biotechnology. When government scientists and government industries launched the Apollo space crafts that put men on the moon, when government-developed and produced ballistic missiles terrorized the Soviets and government-designed and operated bombers bombed the Reds in Korea and

---

[40] Isabel Kershner, "Israeli venture meant to serve electric cars ending its run," *New York Times,* May 27, 2013. Ronald D. White, "One owner, low miles, will finance: sellers try to unload Fiskers," *Los Angeles Times,* April 26, 2013. Rachel Feintzeig, "Electric-car maker Coda files for bankruptcy," *Wall Street Journal*, May 1, 2013.

Vietnam to "contain communism" and secure American dominance of the Free World for corporate subscribers of the *Wall Street Journal* to exploit – where then was the *cri de coeur* that "government can't pick winners"? And what about those government-run drones? Anti-government big-mouth Rand Paul filibustered for a whole day against the threat of swarms of government drones over American cities, but I didn't hear him complain that government drones *don't work.* That wasn't his problem. And when, after an *eight-year long* mind-bogglingly difficult, complex and risky 150 *million-mile* journey, NASA's government-built *Curiosity* space ship landed a (government-built) state-of-the-art science lab the size of a Mini Cooper within a mile and a half of its target on the surface of *Mars*, and then immediately set off to explore its new neighborhood, even the Ayn Rand-loving government-hating Republicans in Congress were awed into silence. As David Sirota's headline in *Salon.com* read on August 13, 2012 just after *Curiosity* set down on the red planet: "Lesson from Mars: Government works!" And right now, as I'm writing this in April 2013, most of a year later, that government-run Mars explorer is happily roving around drilling core samples to find out if there is now or used to be, water and possibly even life on Mars – this while back home, Shell Oil's private capitalist-run arctic drilling platform ran aground in an arctic storm and is now being towed away to Asia for repairs while Shell Oil's shareholders are having second thoughts about their CEO's wisdom in "picking winners" by squandering $5 billion on this fool's errand of drilling for oil under Artic ice.[41]

One planet, one people, one economy for the common good

For better or worse, we are well into what scientists call the "Anthropocene". Nature doesn't run Earth anymore. We do. So if we are, after all, just "one people on one planet", it's time we begin to make conscious *and collective* decisions about how our economic activity affects the natural world – and I don't mean "geoengineering" the planet by wrapping glaciers in tin foil to slow their melting while capitalism goes right on cooking and pillaging the planet. Since the rise of capitalism 300 years ago, more and more of the world has come to be run on the principle of *market anarchy*, on Adam Smith's maxim that every individual should just maximize his/her own interest – "look out for number 1" – and the "public interest", the "common good"

---

[41] Kenneth Chang, "Mars could have supported life long ago, NASA says," *New York Times*, March 12, 2013. And Shell Oil isn't the only company having second thoughts about what it's brilliant CEO thought was a sure thing: Clifford Krauss, "ConocoPhilips suspends its Arctic drilling plans, *New York Times*, April 11, 2013.

would take care of itself. Well, that hasn't worked out so well. It was always a dumb theory, but it's worked OK for the 1% who could mostly manage without the commons. For the rest of us, the more capitalism, the more the common good gets trashed. And now globalized market anarchy is destroying not just humanity and society but even life on Earth.[42] The problem with Smith's theory is that the aggregate of private interests don't add up to the public interest. The problems we face with respect to the planetary environment and ecology can't be solved by individual choice in the marketplace. It requires:

- *collective democratic control over the economy to prioritize the needs of society, the environment, other species and future generations*;
- *local, national and global economic planning to reorganize the world economy and redeploy labor and resources to these ends;*
- an economy of *guaranteed full employment* because if we would have to shut down ExxonMobil and GM and Monsanto[43] and Walmart and so on to save the world, then we have to provide equal or better jobs for all those laid off workers because otherwise they won't support what we all need to do to save ourselves.

Ecosocialism and the salvation of small businesses

This does *not at all* mean that we would have to nationalize local restaurants, family farms, farmers markets, artisans, groceries, bakeries, repair shops, workers co-ops and the like. Small-scale, self-managed producers based on simple reproduction are

---

[42] Citing a recent study by an international team of researchers in *Nature Climate Change* in May 2013, the BBC reports that if "rapid action" is not taken to curb greenhouse gases, some 34% of animals and 57% of plants will lose more than half of their current habitat ranges. Dr. Rachel Warren, the lead scientist of the study said that "Our research predicts that climate change will greatly reduce the diversity of even very common species found in most parts of the world. This loss of global-scale biodiversity would significantly impoverish the biosphere and the ecosystem services it provides. There will also be a knock-on effect for humans because these species are important for things like water and air purification, flood control, nutrient cycling, and eco-tourism." Matt McGrath, "'Dramatic decline' warning for plants and animals," *BBC News Online*, May 12, 2013 at http://www.bbc.co.uk/news/science-environment-22500673.

[43] On the existential threat Monsanto Corporation poses to humanity and the planet, see the Green Shadow Cabinet: "What must be done about Monsanto corporation, and why." May 23, 2013 at
http://greenshadowcabinet.us/statements/ecology-what-must-be-done-about-monsanto-corporation-and-why.

not destroying the world. Large-scale capitalist investor-owned corporations based on insatiable accumulation *are* destroying the world. So they would have to be nationalized, many closed down, others scaled back, others repurposed. But an ecosocialist society would rescue and promote small-scale, local self-managed businesses because we would need them, indeed, we would want many more of them whereas, today, capitalism is driving them out of business everywhere.

4. Rational planning requires democracy: voting the big questions

Solar or coal? Frack the planet or work our way off fossil fuels? Drench the world's farms in toxic pesticides or return to organic agriculture. Public transportation or private cars as the mainstay? Let's put the big questions up for a vote. Shouldn't everyone have a say in decisions that affect them all? Isn't that the essential idea of democracy? The problem with capitalism is that the economy isn't up for a vote. But it needs to be. Again, in Adam Smith's day it mattered less, at least for the environment, because private decisions had so little impact on the planet. But today, huge decisions that affect all of us, other species, and even the fate of life on Earth, *are all still private decisions,* made by corporate boards on behalf of self-interested investors.

Polls show that 57% of Chinese feel that protecting the environment should be given priority, even at the expense of economic growth, and only 21% prioritize the economy over the environment.[44] But, obviously, the Chinese don't get to vote on that or anything else. Polls show Americans opposed to GMO foods outnumber supporters nearly two to one, and 82% of Americans favor labeling of GMO foods.[45] But Americans don't get to vote on whether we get GMOs in our food or get told about it. Well, why not? Corporate boards vote to put GMOs and all kinds of toxic chemicals in our food. We're the ones who consume this stuff. We can't avoid GMOs simply by refusing to purchase them – the "market solution" – because they're everywhere, they're in 80% of the foods we consume, and Monsanto and the rest of the GMO industrial complex bribe politicians and regulators with campaign

---

[44] Gallup, June 8, 2012 at: http://www.gallup.com/poll/155102/majority-chinese-prioritize-environment-economy.aspx.
[45] *Huffington Post*, "GMO poll finds huge majority say foods should be labeled," March 4, 2013 at:
http://www.huffingtonpost.com/2013/03/04/gmo-poll_n_2807595.html.

contributions and lucrative revolving-door jobs to make sure you don't know what foods to avoid.[46] Well, why should we accept this? Why shouldn't we have a say in these decisions? We don't have to be experts; corporate boards aren't composed of experts. They're mainly comprised of major investors. They discuss and vote on what they want to do, then hire experts to figure out how to implement their decisions. Why can't we do that – for humanity's interests?

Every cook can govern

From Tunisa to Tahir Square, Zacotti Park to Gezi Park, Madison Wisconsin to Kunming Yunnan, Songjian Shanghai, Shifang Sichuan, Guangzhou and thousands of sites and cities and towns all over China, ordinary citizens demonstrate remarkably rational environmental sense against the profit-driven environmental irrationality and irresponsibility of their rulers.[47] In Turkey, "Sultan" Erdogon's decree to tear up Istanbul's last major park to replace it with an Ottoman-style shopping mall provoked mass outrage. Protestors complained, as one put it: "When were we asked what we wanted? We have three times as many mosques as we do schools. Yet they are building new mosques. There are eight shopping malls in the vicinity of Taksim, yet they want to build another... Where are the opera houses? The theatres? The culture and youth centers? What about those? They only choose what will bring them the most profit without considering what we need."[48] When, in a bid to mollify the protestors, a spokesman for the ruling Justice and Development Party (AKP) floated the excellent idea of a public referendum on the issue saying: "We might put it to a referendum... In democracies the will of the people counts". Erdogon considered this option for a moment but when protestors doubted his sincerity, he proved them right by calling in his riot squads to crush the protests instead.[49]

---

[46] See again, Green Shadow Cabinet, "What must be done about Monsanto, and why?" op cit.
[47] E.g., Jennifer Duggan, "Kunming pollution is the tip of rising Chinese environmental activism," *Guardian* blog post May 16, 2013 at 11.59EDT at http://www.guardian.co.uk/environment/chinas-choice/2013/may/16/kunming-pollution-protest-chinese-environmental-activism.
[48] Tim Arango and Ceylan Yeginsu, "Peaceful protest over Istanbul park turns violent as police crack down," *New York Times*, May 31, 2013.
[49] "Turkish government moots referendum on Gezi Park," *Deutsche Welle,* June 12, 2013 at: http://www.dw.de/turkish-government-moots-referendum-on-gezi-park/a-16877383.

In Brazil, on the heels of the Turkish protests, mass protests erupted over announced bus fare hikes but soon morphed into more sweeping social protest as hundreds of thousands of Brazilians turned out in cities across the country to denounce the irresponsible waste of public funds on extravagant soccer stadiums in the run-up to the World Cup in 2014 when schools, public transportation, hospitals, health care and other public services are neglected: "People are going hungry and the government builds stadiums," said Eleuntina Scuilgaro, a pensioner. "I love soccer, but we need schools" said Evaldir Cardoso, a firemen at a protest with his seven-month old son. "These protests are in favor of common sense", argued protestor Roberta da Matta, "We pay an absurd amount of taxes in Brazil, and now more people are questioning what they are getting in return."[50]

If corporations and capitalist governments can't align production with the common good and ecological rationality, what other choice is there but for society to collectively and democratically organize, plan and manage most production themselves? To do this we would have to establish democratic institutions to plan and manage our social economy. We would have to set up planning boards at local, regional, national/continental and international levels. Those would have to include not just workers, the direct producers, but entire communities, consumers, farmers, peasants, everyone. We have models: the Paris Commune, Russian soviets, Brazil's participatory planning, La Via Campesina, and others. Direct democracy at the base, delegated authority with right of recall for higher level planning boards. What's so difficult about that?

The example of public regulation of public utilities

As Greg Palast, Jarrold Oppenheim and Theo MacGregor described in *Democracy and Regulation: How the Public Can Govern Essential Services* (2003), it is a curious and ironic fact that the United States, foremost protagonist of the free market, possesses a large and indispensable sector of the economy that is not governed by the free market but instead, democratically, by public oversight – and that is utilities: the provision of electricity, heating fuel, water and sewerage, and local telephone service. Not only that, but these are the most efficient and cheapest utility systems in the world. The authors note that British residents pay 44 percent more for electricity than do American consumers, 85 percent more for local

---

[50] Simon Romero, "Protests grow as Brazilians blame leaders," *New York Times*, June 19, 2013.

telephone service and 26 percent more for natural gas. Europeans pay even more, Latin Americans more than Europeans. They write that:

> "Americans pay astonishingly little for high-quality public services, yet low charges do not suppress wages: American utility workers are the nation's industrial elite, with a higher concentration of union membership than in any other private industry."

Palast, Oppenheim and MacGregor attribute this to the fact that, unlike Britain and most of the rest of the world, utilities are not unregulated free-market corporations like ExxonMobil or Monsanto or Rio Light or British Water. Instead, they are tightly regulated industries, mostly privately owned, but many publicly owned by local municipalities. Yet even when utilities are privately owned like Con Edison in New York or Green Mountain Power in Vermont or Florida Power and Light (to take some east coast examples), it's really hard to call this "capitalism". It's more like state capitalism, even quasi-socialism. Either way, public or investor owned, they are highly regulated, subject to public oversight, involvement and control:

> "Unique in the world (with the exception of Canada), every aspect of US regulation is wide open to the public. There are no secret meetings, no secret documents. Any and all citizens and groups are invited to take part: individuals, industrial customers, government agencies, consumer groups, trade unions, the utility itself, even its competitors. *Everyone affected by the outcome has a right to make their case openly, to ask questions of government and utilities, to read all financial and operating records in detail.* In public forums, with all information open to all citizens, the principles of social dialogue and transparency come to life. It is an extra-ordinary exercise in democracy – and it works... Another little known fact is that, despite the recent experiments with markets in electricity [the authors published this book in 2003, just three years after the Enron privatization debacle], the US holds to the strictest, most elaborate and detailed system of regulation anywhere: private utilities' profits are capped, investments directed or vetoed by public agencies. Privately owned utilities are directed to reduce prices for the poor, fund environmentally

157

friendly physical and financial inspection... Americans, while
strongly attached to private property and ownership, demand stern
and exacting government control over vital utility services."[51]

The authors are careful to note that this is "no regulatory Garden of Eden". It has
many failings: regulation is constantly under attack by promoters of market pricing,
the public interest and the profit motive of investor-owned utilities often conflict
with negative consequences for the public, and so on.[52] But even so, this long-

---

[51] Greg Palast, Jerrold Oppenheim, and Theo MacGregor, *Democracy and Regulation: How
the Public can Govern Essential Services* (London: Pluto, 2003) pp. 2-4, my italics. The
authors point out yet another irony of this system of public regulation, namely that it was
created by *private companies* as the lesser evil to fend off the threat of nationalization:
"Modern US utility regulation is pretty much the invention of American Telephone &
Telegraph Company (AT&T) and the National Electric Light Association (NELA) – the
investor-owned telephone and electric industries at the turn of the twentieth century. They
saw regulation as protection against Populist and Progressive movements that, since the
economic panic of 1873 and later disruptions, had galvanized anti-corporate farmer and labor
organizations. By the turn of the twentieth century, these movements had galvanized
considerable public support for governmental ownership of utilities... " p. 98.
[52] In the case of nuclear power plants, local public regulation has often been subverted and
overridden by the federal government in its zealous drive to push nuclear power even against
the wishes of the local public. Thus in the aftermath of the Three Mile Island nuclear accident
in 1979, social scientists Raymond Goldsteen and John Schorr interviewed residents around
Three Mile Island about the history of the power plant, why it was built, what voice they had
in the decision to build it, and about the decision to restart the plant after the accident. It turns
out that, as one resident, a Mrs. Kelsey put it, they had no choice. They were virtually forced
to accept it: "They [Met Ed the utility, and the Nuclear Regulatory Commission] keep saying
we need this nuclear. They keep pounding that into our heads with the news and everything.
We need it. We need it. We can't do without it." Residents told Goldstein and Schorr that the
surrounding communities petitioned against restarting the plant after the accident but lost
again. Another resident, Mrs. Boswell, said" We don't want to be guinea pigs... I still think
that we should have a say, too, in what goes on. I really do, because we're the victims." Mrs.
Brown: "The company just wants [to reopen the plant for] the money... " Mrs. Carmen: "No,
they're going to do what they want... I don't think [community feelings] would bother them at
all." Mrs. Hemmingway: "I feel very angry about it really, because I just feel that there is so
much incompetence on the part of the utility, on the part of the NRC, on the part of the local
governments..." Residents said that if they had been honestly informed about the risks, and if
they had had a choice, they would have investigated other technologies, and chosen
differently. Mrs. Hemingway again: "It just seems to me there are so many alternatives we
could explore... We obviously need alternate energy sources, but solar could provide heating
for houses and water [and so on]." Residents said they would have preferred other choices
even if it meant giving up certain conveniences: Mrs. Caspar: "I don't really mind conserving
all that much. If people can conserve gas [for cars] why can't they conserve energy? Now I
don't mean I want to go back to the scrubboard... But I don't dry my clothes in the dryer. I
hang them... on the line. . . and I do try to conserve as far as that goes." (pp. 181-183,212).
One of the most interesting results of this study, which is well worth reading in full, is that it

established and indisputably successful example of democratic public regulation of large-scale industries offers us a real-world practical example of something like a "proto-socialism". I see no obvious reason something like this model of democracy and transparency could not be extended, expanded, fully socialized, and replicated to encompass the entire large-scale industrial economy. Of course, as I argued above, to save the humans, we would have to do much more than just "regulate" industries. We would have to completely reorganize and reprioritize the whole economy – indeed the whole global industrial economy. This means not just regulating but retrenching and closing down resource-consuming and polluting industries, shifting resources out of them, starting up new industries and so on. Those are huge tasks, beyond the scope of even the biggest corporations, even many governments. So who else could do this but self-organized masses of citizens, the whole society acting in concert, democratically? Obviously, many issues can be decided at local levels. Others, like closing down the coal industry or repurposing the auto industry, require large-scale planning at national if not international levels. Some, like global warming, ocean acidification, deforestation – would require extensive international coordination, virtually global planning. I don't see why that's not doable. We have the UN Climate Convention which meets annually and is charged with regulating GHG emissions. It fails to do so only because it lacks enforcement powers. We need to give it enforcement powers.

5. Democracy can only work in context of rough socio-economic equality and social guarantees

When in the midst of the Great Depression, the great "people's jurist" Supreme Court Justice Louis Brandeis said *"We can either have democracy in this country or we can have great wealth concentrated in the hands of a few, but we can't have both"*, he was more right than he knew. Today we have by far the greatest concentration of wealth in history. So it's hardly surprising that we have the weakest

---

illustrates how ordinary citizens, given the chance, would make more rational decisions about technology, safety, and the environment than the "experts" at the utility, Met Ed, and the Nuclear Regulatory Commission. It's not that they were more knowledgeable about the technology than the experts but that the experts were not impartial. They were representing the industry and profits and the NRC, not the public, *so they could not help but systematically make wrong decisions*, decisions that in this case not only violated the public trust and but put huge numbers of lives in danger. Raymond L. Goldsteen and John K. Schorr, *Demanding Democracy After Three Mile Island* (Gainsville: University of Florida Press 1991).

and most corrupt democracies since the Gilded Age. If we want democracy, we would have to abolish "the great wealth concentrated in the hands of the few". That means abolishing not just private property in the means of production, but also extremes of income, exorbitant salaries, great property and inheritance. Because *the only way to prevent corruption of democracy is to make it impossible to materially gain by doing so* – by creating a society with neither rich nor poor, a society of basic economic equality.

Does that mean we would all have to dress in blue Mao suits and dine in communal mess halls? Hardly. Lots of studies (Wilkinson and Pickett's *Spirit Level*, the UK's *New Economics Foundation* studies and others) have shown that people are happier, there's less crime and violence and fewer mental health problems in societies where income differences are small and where concentrated wealth is limited. We don't have five planets to provide the resources for the whole world to live the "American Dream" of endless consumerism. But we have more than enough wealth to provide every human being on the planet with a basic income, with a good job at pay sufficient to lead a dignified life, with safe water and sanitation, quality food, housing, education and healthcare, with public transportation – all the *authentic* necessities we really need. These should all be guaranteed *as a matter of right*, as indeed most of these were already declared as such in the Universal Declaration of Human Rights of 1948.

Freeing ourselves from the toil of producing unnecessary and/or harmful commodities – *the three quarters of current U.S. production that's a waste* – would free us to shorten the work day, to enjoy the leisure promised but never delivered by capitalism, to *redefine the meaning of the standard of living to connote a way of life that is actually richer, while consuming less,* to realize our fullest human potential instead of wasting our lives in mindless drudgery and shopping. This is the emancipatory promise of ecosocialism.

The Universal Declaration of Human Rights

Article 22
Everyone, as a member of society, has the right to social security and is entitled to realization, through national effort and international co-operation and in accordance with the organization and resources of each State, of the economic, social and cultural

rights indispensable for his dignity and the free development of his personality.

Article 23
(1) Everyone has the right to work, to free choice of employment, to just and favourable conditions of work and to protection against unemployment.
(2) Everyone, without any discrimination, has the right to equal pay for equal work.
(3) Everyone who works has the right to just and favourable remuneration ensuring for himself and his family an existence worthy of human dignity, and supplemented, if necessary, by other means of social protection.
(4) Everyone has the right to form and to join trade unions for the protection of his interests.

Article 24
Everyone has the right to rest and leisure, including reasonable limitation of working hours and periodic holidays with pay.

Article 25
(1) Everyone has the right to a standard of living adequate for the health and well-being of himself and of his family, including food, clothing, housing and medical care and necessary social services, and the right to security in the event of unemployment, sickness, disability, widowhood, old age or other lack of livelihood in circumstances beyond his control.
(2) Motherhood and childhood are entitled to special care and assistance. All children, whether born in or out of wedlock, shall enjoy the same social protection.

6. This is crazy, utopian, impossible, never happen

Perhaps. But what's the alternative? The spectre of planet-wide ecological collapse and the collapse of civilization into some kind of *Bladerunner* dystopia is not as hypothetical as it once seemed. Ask the Chinese. China's "capitalist miracle" has already driven that country off the cliff into headlong ecological collapse that threatens to take the whole planet down with it. With virtually all its rivers and lakes polluted and many depleted, with 70% of its croplands contaminated with heavy metals and other toxins, with undrinkable water, inedible food, unbreathable air that kills more than a million Chinese a year, with "cancer villages" metastasizing over the rural landscape and cancer the leading cause of death in Beijing,[53] China's rulers face hundreds of mass protests, often violent, around the country every day, more than a hundred thousand protest a year, and even with all their police-state instruments of repression, they know they can't keep the lid on forever. Indeed, hundreds of thousands of Communist Party kleptocrats can see the writing on the wall through the smog and are moving their families, their money and themselves out of the country before it's too late. Today the Chinese, and we ourselves, need a socialist revolution not just to abolish exploitation and alienation, but to derail the capitalist train wreck of ecological collapse before it takes us all over the edge. As China itself demonstrates, revolutions come and go. Economic systems come and go. Capitalism has had a 300-year run. The question is: will humanity stand by and let the world be destroyed to save the profit system?

The spectre of eco-democratic revolution

That outcome depends to a great extent on whether we on the left can answer that question "what's your alternative?" with a compelling and plausible vision of an eco-socialist civilization – and figure out how to get there. We have our work cut out for us. But what gives the growing global eco-socialist movement an edge in this ideological struggle is that capitalism has *no solution to the ecological* crisis, *no way to put the brakes on collapse*, because its only answer to every problem is more of the same growth that's killing us.

"History" was supposed to have "ended" with the fall of communism and the triumph of capitalism two decades ago. Yet today, history is very much alive and it is, ironically, capitalism itself which is being challenged more broadly than ever and found wanting for solutions. Today, we are very much living in one of those pivotal, world-changing moments in history – indeed it is no exaggeration to say that this is *the* most critical moment in human history.

---

[53] Edward Wong, "Air pollution linked to 1.2 million premature deaths in China," *New York Times*. April 1, 2013. Johnathan Kaiman, "Inside China's 'cancer villages,'" *Guardian*, June 4, 2012.

Capitalism and destruction of life on Earth: six theses on saving the humans

We may be fast approaching the precipice of ecological collapse, but the means to derail this trainwreck are in the making as, around the world, struggles against the destruction of nature, against dams, against pollution, against overdevelopment, against the siting of chemical plants and power plants, against predatory resource extraction, against the imposition of GMOs, against privatization of remaining common lands, water and public services, against capitalist unemployment and *precarité* are growing and building momentum. Today we're riding a swelling wave of near simultaneous global mass democratic "awakening" – almost global mass uprising. This global insurrection is still in its infancy, still unsure of its future, but its radical democratic instincts are, I believe, humanity's last best hope.

Let's make history!

CPSIA information can be obtained
at www.ICGtesting.com
Printed in the USA
FSOW02n2033280716
23230FS